Drug Development Programme Management

Barbara Ann Lead

Interpharm Press
Denver, Colorado

Library of Congress Cataloging-in-Publication Data

Lead, Barbara Ann.
Drug development programme management.
p. ; cm.
Includes bibliographical references and index.
ISBN 1-57491-111-2
1. Drug development—Management. I. Title.
[DNLM: 1. Drug Industry—organization & administration. 2. Drug Approval. 3. Research Design. QV 736 L434d 2000]
RM301.25 L43 2000
615′.19—dc21

00-031941

10 9 8 7 6 5 4 3 2 1

ISBN: 1-57491-111-2

Commissioned in Europe by Sue Horwood of Medi-Tech. Publications, Storrington, England, on behalf of Interpharm Press, Denver, Colorado, USA. General Scientific Advisor: Dr. Guy Wingate, UK Quality Manager, Computer Systems Compliance, Secondary Manufacturing, Glaxo Wellcome, Barnard Castle, England.

Interpharm Press
15 Inverness Way E.
Englewood, CO 80112-5776, USA

Phone: +1-303-662-9101
Fax: +1-303-754-3953
Orders/on-line catalog:
www.interpharm.com

Contents

Preface

The pharmaceutical industry is currently undergoing change at an ever-increasing pace. The latest mergers between Astra and Zeneca and Hoechst Marion Rousell and Rhône Poulenc Rorer are but more examples of the rapid changes being brought about by the need to increase shareholder value. One of the drivers for such mergers is to increase the ability of research and development (R&D) to bring innovative products to the market, since this is what is required to grow profits as patents expire, development costs escalate and competition intensifies.

This book discusses how programme management and related systems and tools can be applied to improve the effectiveness and productivity of development and to reduce time to market. Part one covers strategic planning and portfolio management. Some examples are provided of simple tools that can be used to select a balanced development portfolio. Resource management for the development portfolio is also discussed, and some approaches are described for the purpose of management. Part two covers project management. I use experience gained over 20 years in the industry to illustrate the critical success factors for high quality, rapid product development and commercialisation.

A broad view of project management is taken, and aspects of ways of working, setting target profiles and other acceptance criteria are discussed. The U.S. Food and Drug Administration (FDA) has stated that more than 25 percent of all clinical trials fail to meet their objectives due to poor trial design. Over 25 percent of all New Drug Applications (NDAs) are returned to the submitting company because of inadequacies in the dossier. Good project management systems should prevent this high rejection rate. Project management should ensure that project plans and strategies are developed in such a way as to provide a competitive product that reaches the market in the shortest time. Development time-scales cannot be minimised unless the quality of the work done is sufficient to secure rapid regulatory approvals.

My experience in the role that the project team must play in providing high quality programmes to minimise time is described in this book. In particular, the importance of good experimental design, setting acceptance criteria, teamwork and problem solving are discussed in relation to the role they can play in reducing development times and maximising the returns from new products.

One important and often neglected aspect of project management is project leadership. Project leadership is somewhat underdeveloped in the industry. Some companies are better than others, but there is often an overemphasis on *management* and an underemphasis on *leadership*. Project management can put too much importance on the development of extremely detailed project plans, Gantt charts, project team meetings and the mechanism of planning, while neglecting the areas of development strategies, setting acceptance criteria, problem solving, continuous improvement in ways of working, risk analysis and contingency planning.

Chapter 10 covers the topic of leadership at some length. Leadership is the ability of an individual to develop a high-achieving team and to empower individual members to give of their very best. In this sense, the style and the roles of some key players need to change, including senior R&D and business managers and project leaders.

It is the role of senior R&D and business managers to provide an environment in which project teams can be high achievers. They must not be a hindrance to progress. Inappropriate micro management is evident in many companies, since many senior managers do not understand the difference between management and leadership.

Leaders set direction and goals and inspire teams to be creative in their achievement. All too often, function heads make decisions (usually with incomplete data) which should be made by the project teams, or they impose inappropriate or unnecessary constraints. A common mistake is a drive for early regulatory filing dates instead of driving toward successful launches which maximise sales and profits. Project teams that are measured by time to regulatory filings will often neglect those aspects of product positioning and differentiation, which are required for successful product launches and maximising sales and profits. Time to market is critical, but time to peak sales is the most important measure.

The case studies in Chapter 12 illustrate some of the points raised concerning leadership, teamwork and ways of working and problem solving. These are areas in which substantial benefits can be obtained if sufficient emphasis is placed on them.

The systems and tools described here are pragmatic and easy to implement but do require management commitment for control. The chapters of this book have been written to provide help and guidance on a specific topic and stand alone for reference purposes. Therefore, it is not necessary to read it in any particular order.

Barbara Ann Lead
July 2000

AUTHOR BIOGRAPHY

Barbara Ann Lead's career in the pharmaceutical industry began in the field of analytical chemistry. She has had wide and varied experience in both line management and project management in Technical Operations, Research and Development and Industrialisation.

In Research and Development, Ms. Lead has been a project leader and also established a department for portfolio and programme management. While employed at Fisons in the Technical Operations Department, she established a project management function and introduced programme management and project management systems for Fisons' facilities in the United Kingdom, the United States and France. Later, Ms. Lead was assigned to a Brazilian subsidiary of Fisons, where she managed the technology transfer of sterile products into manufacturing and established a Quality Assurance Department.

In January 1997, Ms. Lead joined Rhône Poulenc Rorer in the United States and was responsible for the Industrialisation Department. In this position, she was responsible for the technology transfer of a range of products into a number of manufacturing facilities in both North and South America.

Early in 1999, Ms. Lead joined Orion Pharma of Finland as Vice President of Respiratory Business, where she is responsible for the development and marketing of a range of products. She now lives in Helsinki.

During her varied career, Ms. Lead has been involved with many different types of projects, and her role within these projects has ranged from team member to project leader to steering group member. She has drawn from this wide experience base to write this book.

Part One

STRATEGIC PLANNING AND DEVELOPMENT PORTFOLIO MANAGEMENT

Management of the research and development (R&D) portfolio is the key to sustaining profit growth in line with the expectations of financial markets. Investors expect to see earnings growth in excess of 10 percent per year, whilst realistic targets for even the largest companies are in the range of 7 to 8 percent growth in earnings. The loss of revenues from blockbuster products to generic competition has been a significant factor for many companies over the last few years, and this trend is set to continue. The selection of innovative drug candidates with clear therapeutic advantages and effective resource management to ensure speed to market without compromising the quality of development programmes are the key management challenges for the next few years.

Resource management is particularly important; the pressure for speed to market often results in project teams omitting important studies, which leave gaps in regulatory dossiers. In 1998, over 25 percent of New Drug Applications (NDAs) were returned to the companies concerned due to deficiencies in the dossiers. Clearly, speed to market is critical, but sufficient resources must be allocated to projects to enable the development and submission of high-quality dossiers that can be approved in the shortest period of time.

Part One includes some simple tools and techniques for improving portfolio management and resource management. The need to understand and manage risk in an innovative portfolio is also discussed.

1

Pressures on the Industry

The key to success in the future for pharmaceutical companies lies as it did in the past—in successful research and development (R&D) producing a steady flow of new products. However, the pressures and difficulties are different from those of as little as 10 years ago. In a rapidly changing environment, the current pressures (Figure 1.1) on our industry include the following:

- Increased costs of R&D
- Innovation more difficult
- Price controls
- Patent expiry
- Effects of competition
- Increasing regulatory requirements

- Shareholder expectations for continued record profit growth

COSTS OF RESEARCH AND DEVELOPMENT ARE INCREASING

Current estimates for the cost to market a New Chemical Entity (NCE) vary according to sources, from U.S.$400 million to U.S.$600 million. This range compares with an estimate of approximately $200 million 10 years ago.

This increase is due to a number of factors, including such issues as increasing regulatory requirements, which requires more studies to be undertaken (see below). The development of innovative compounds is becoming more complex. For example, clinical programmes in chronic degenerative diseases require endpoints to be measured which are not straightforward, and the complexity of undertaking health status (quality of life) and health economic studies for regulatory and re-imbursement purposes is increasing.

The U.S. Food and Drug Administration (FDA) requirement for pre-approval inspections requires more work to be done on the commercial manufacturing process earlier in development. In the case of a drug substance, substantial investment in the plant can be required before proof of efficacy and safety has been demonstrated.

INNOVATION IS BECOMING MORE DIFFICULT

The success of the past 40 years has meant that novelty is more difficult to achieve. Current areas of unmet need, e.g., stroke, Alzheimer's disease, AIDS (acquired immunodeficiency syndrome), multiple sclerosis and so on, are proving more difficult and expensive to discover significant compounds. For instance, stroke effects a large number of patients every year, but it is a difficult area in which to undertake clinical research, since diagnosis

Figure 1.1. Pressures on the Pharmaceutical Industry

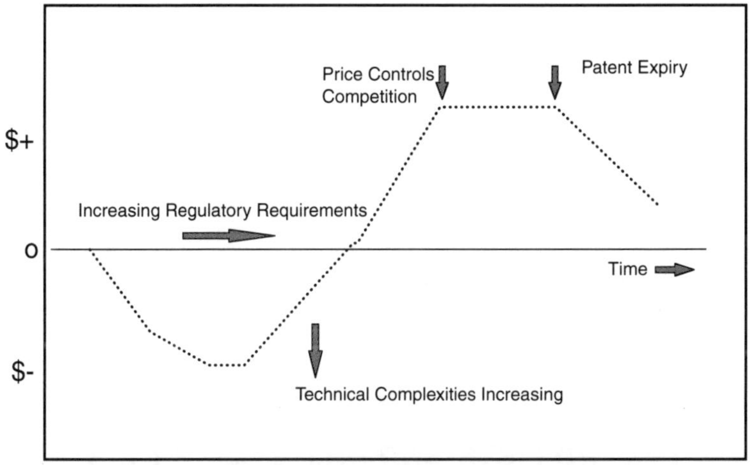

is often made several hours or even days following the initial event. This reduces the availability of suitable patients for clinical research, resulting in elongated development times, which makes clinical research very difficult.

Similar difficulties were experienced with the development of compounds for acute myocardial infarction until a significant breakthrough was discovered which showed that the damage to the myocardium could be minimised if patients were treated within 4 hours of the infarction. This discovery changed medical practice and, in turn, made research into more effective treatments easier by providing earlier access to a larger number of patients.

Asthma is a therapy area in which many compounds have been successfully developed and commercialised, but there remains a need for better preventive treatments. Oral prophylactic therapy includes compounds such as corticosteroids, theophyllines, leukotriene antagonists and so on. Corticosteroids and theophyllines have significant systemic side effects associated with oral administration, and the leukotriene antagonists are not effective in all patients; typically less than 30 percent of asthmatics will respond to these compounds. The systemic side effects of corticosteroids are reduced by topical administration to the lung, but this route requires the use of inhaler devices, which can be difficult for patients to use correctly, thus leading to poor compliance.

Asthma is not a homogeneous disease, and its causes are not really understood. There are no animal models for asthma, and there are no diagnostic tests for the different asthmatic subtypes. This makes discovery and development of new compounds, which will have significant advantages over current therapies, very difficult and, since efficacy cannot be predicted without patient studies, costly.

LIMITED LISTS AND PRICE CONTROLS

Healthcare systems around the world are finding costs spiralling, and price controls on pharmaceuticals are becoming increasingly stringent. Healthcare providers increasingly are prepared to pay premium prices only for products that are cost-effective. They must either provide significant therapeutic advantages over existing ones or reduce the total healthcare cost for the patient.

In order to demonstrate reduced total treatment costs, companies must undertake pharmaco-economic studies. These studies are often expensive to perform and can include long-term assessment of patients, which adds to development time-scales and costs.

PATENT EXPIRY

As the patents on the successful compounds of the 1980s expire, more and more novel compounds are required not only to maintain sales and profits but also to continue to provide the growth expected by shareholders. This is a big issue for companies dealing with the expiration of the patent on a blockbuster drug.

EFFECTS OF COMPETITION

As innovation becomes more difficult, more companies are racing to be the first to market with novel compounds in a given therapeutic class. Those companies whose compounds are not in the first three in a class may never recoup their development and launch costs.

Achieving "first in class" 25 years ago usually resulted in a number of years exclusivity before "second" and "third in class" compounds came along. Tagamet® was launched in 1977, and it was 7 years later before Glaxo launched Zantac®; hence, Smith Kline was able to secure considerable sales without direct competition for that time. Today, it is common for "first in class" compounds to have only one or two years before competitors with some therapeutic advantage enter the market. Invirase® was launched in 1995, and a competitor product was launched within 1 year.

INCREASING REGULATORY REQUIREMENTS

Authorities are asking for more information than was the case one or two decades ago. Clinical programmes are under more scrutiny; for instance, surrogate endpoints are being accepted less and less, and quality of life endpoints are asked for in many cases.

More emphasis is being placed on pharmacokinetics and pharmacodynamics, and as the knowledge in these specialities increases, more studies in certain patient populations, e.g., hepatic- and renal-compromised groups are being requested. Also, in the clinical development of compounds used to treat patients on multiple therapies, the costs of laboratory work, including drug interactions, can be extremely expensive.

Pre-approval inspections and the requirements for pivotal clinical studies to be undertaken with product made from the same process as that which will be marketed is causing more capital investment in both primary and secondary manufacturing facilities to be made much earlier in the development process.

This investment is usually required before clinical efficacy is proven, whereas 10 years ago major capital investments in manufacturing were made only when the probability of drug approvals was high.

SHAREHOLDER EXPECTATIONS FOR CONTINUED RECORD PROFIT GROWTH

Pharmaceutical companies have been among the highest performing stocks for many years, stimulated by consistent quality growth in earnings and profits. However, as blockbuster drugs come off patent, as has happened to a number of companies in the last few years, alternative strategies are needed to support continued growth. In addition to organic growth by innovative R&D, many companies have looked toward mergers, acquisitions and other strategic alliances to provide sales grwoth and cost reductions through synergies in a number of areas, including R&D, sales, and marketing and manufacturing.

Acquisitions and mergers, co-development and co-marketing arrangements bring a new level of complexity to the companies involved. Issues such as communications, cultural differences, intercompany management of projects and geographically dispersed project teams have to be faced and resolved. This puts pressure on leaders who need a new set of skills and management tools to be successful in this new and rapidly changing environment.

In the future, the key to successful R&D will require companies to be successful in the following critical areas:

- Innovation
- Time to market
- Management of the development project portfolio
- Leadership of projects

Innovation

The pressures to innovate are substantial, not only in the discovery of new compounds but also in new drug delivery systems and combination therapies. The following factors are additive:

- Shareholders want future sales and profit growth.
- The regulatory approval process favours innovative drugs.
- Limited lists.
- Corporate image.
- Scientists' motivation.
- Pressure groups—breakthrough drugs are required in areas of unmet need (AIDS, multiple sclerosis, etc.).
- Pricing policies favour innovative drugs.

Time to Market

Minimising development times is a critical success factor for all pharmaceutical companies if R&D costs are to be recouped. The majority of companies are addressing this issue, since success in the reduction of development times conveys competitive advantage.

- Sales and profits are maximised from patent protection.
- Opportunity to maximise market share.
- Development costs will be contained.
- Performance compared with the competition is optimised.

Management of the Development Portfolio

Effective management of the development project portfolio can provide a flow of new products to the market in line with the strategic business objectives for profit growth. This management process must include the following elements.

Programme Management

Programme management includes the selection and approval of projects in the development portfolio as well as management and control of individual projects.

Portfolio Selection

Portfolio selection can be complex and requires consideration of the merit of the compound available for development and the relative merit of projects competing for the same resources. An analysis of the following factors is important:

- Development project opportunities
- Risk
- Development strengths
- Balance of risk and potential return
- Balance of number of projects and spending per project—develop fewer compounds or spend less per compound
- Business strategies and plans
- Competition
- Resources

Strategic Decision Making

Figure 1.2 summarises the kinds of decisions that the R&D director and his senior team have to make. These decisions affect the

Figure 1.2. Strategic Decisions

allocation of resources to projects, the flow of new products to the market and, therefore, the long-term performance of the company.

Project Nomination/Cancellation

Before a new project is nominated for development, several issues need to be considered, i.e., potential benefits, risks and resource requirements. A new project may have an impact upon time-scales for current projects if there is competition for a scarce resource. When a project is cancelled, considerable resources, depending on the phase of the project, may become available.

Speed of Project Progress

The decision on how quickly individual projects will be progressed will depend on the

- relative potential benefits of all projects in the portfolio,
- relative risks,
- time to market,
- resources required and
- resources available.

Summary

Project management systems can be applied to all of the above elements that are required for the effective management of the development portfolio. Figure 1.3 summarises the areas in which project management systems can support the management of the R&D portfolio and, hence, the growth of pharmaceutical companies.

In the short term, project management systems can be used to plan projects in the current development portfolio and to report progress. Details will be given in a later chapter. In the medium and longer term, project management systems can be used to provide management information for strategic planning and decision making. Details of how these tools can be used will be given in Chapter 4.

Figure 1.3. Project Management Systems Supporting Growth

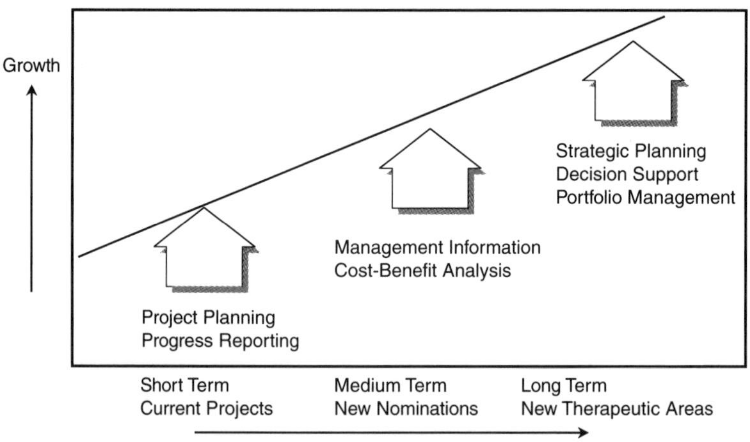

2

Strategic Planning

The development of a strategic plan for research and development (R&D) requires an evaluation of the scientific opportunities available within the framework of the commercial outlook for the business and the availability of resources (see Figure 2.1).

SCIENTIFIC OPPORTUNITIES

An evaluation of the scientific opportunties requires consideration of the following key areas.

Therapeutic Areas of Interest

The development of strategies needs to include consideration of the core strengths of the business, market trends and current project opportunities. Current projects in the research portfolio and future research will be influenced by such issues as, "Does

Figure 2.1. Strategic Planning

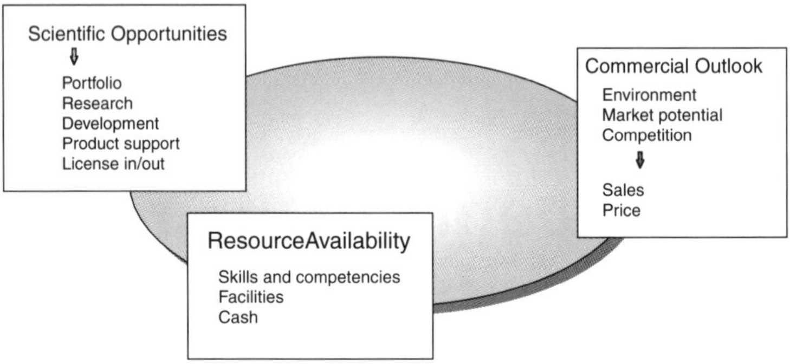

the company want to be a leader or follower in a particular area—to be research lead or market lead" (i.e., the drivers for research are scientifically driven by the skills and interests of the scientists)?

Whether to lead in certain classes or follow a company with an established lead will influence the risk in a portfolio. The development of molecules in an existing class has less risk in terms of predicted efficacy, but speed to market is very important. Following an established lead requires that a compound be number two or at least third to market if essentially similar to the leader, otherwise a significant advantage in efficacy, safety or cost will be required. In these cases, speed to market is even more critical than for a truly innovative product, and the development programme must clearly identify the advantages over existing therapies for product positioning and differentiation.

Whether the research portfolio is research or market driven may vary with the therapeutic category. If a company is research lead, screening and candidate selection will be based on the potential merits of a compound alone. Here the interests, skills and competencies of the research staff will dictate the portfolio. Subsequently, development programmes will be dictated by the types of compounds that are discovered in research, and resources allocated accordingly.

In therapeutic areas where there is substantial unmet clinical need (diseases of old age, viral infections, asthma, COPD, cancer etc.), research lead strategies may be considered most appropriate. In therapeutic areas such as cardiovascular and certain respiratory diseases, where there are substantial numbers of therapies available, a more market lead approach may be most appropriate.

If a company is a market leader, research programmes will be driven by market gap analysis. This often means that the Marketing Department will be more involved with the planning of the research programmes and the selection of candidates for development. However, being a market leader does not mean that the marketing function decides the portfolio. There are many examples in the past where marketing functions have had less understanding of market gaps than the research scientists and the medical staff. The development of Tagamet®, Zantac® and many other compounds were driven by market lead strategies developed by R&D, not the Marketing Department of the companies involved.

Decisions are often iterative, in that at any point in time the strategy can be influenced by the availability of good candidates coming out of discovery, since screens used in research may identify a potential compound in an area that is outside the current strategy. Conversely, the failure of candidates in development may influence a decision to move away from a therapeutic area or class previously of interest or even considered as a core competency.

In summary, the choice of which therapeutic areas a company wants to be in is influenced by a number of factors:

- Company strategic business plan
- Business growth targets
- Core competencies
- Range and value of marketed products
- Understanding of the commercial outlook

Balance Between Research, Development and Product Support for Resource Allocation

A consideration for the strategic plan is what balance is required between research, development and product support projects and depends on a number of factors, including the following:

- Business strategy for the number of New Chemical Entities (NCEs) to be launched each year
- Business strategy for the number of therapeutic areas to be included in core business
- The number of suitable compounds available for development
- The number of marketed products which contribute 80 percent of the company profits (The larger this number is, the larger the potential number of product support projects.)
- The position in the product life cycle for the marketed products contributing 80 percent of company profits
- Company strategy for product life-cycle management
- In/out licence strategies and opportunities

This balance will affect the funding required and will therefore have an impact on the R&D budget.

The size of research spending is usually dictated by long-term business objectives. The proportion of development spending between NCEs and product support such as line extensions and new presentations can most usefully be dictated by the status of the development portfolio with respect to the number of NCEs which meet the criteria for continuing development. Line extension projects aimed at increasing the sales of marketed products and extending product life cycles can be introduced as resources are available or as appropriate to manage risk.

Licence In and Out

Licensing strategies will depend on opportunities available; the gaps in the development portfolio with respect to the match with business objectives (licence in); and the match between project opportunities, strategic fit or funds available for development (licence out).

RESOURCE AVAILABILITY

The resources available largely determine the extent to which the opportunities discussed above can be realised. Resources include the skills and experience of the staff, facilities and equipment available and budget or cash flow requirements.

THE R&D BUDGET

Setting the R&D budget for many companies is achieved by allocating a percentage of sales revenue. Most companies spend between 10 percent and 20 percent of their total sales—the exact amount depending on a balance between the status of the R&D portfolio and the profit targets of the business.

Companies require a steady flow of NCEs to the market if growth is to be sustained. In particular, as patents expire on marketed products and revenues are eroded by generic competition, new products are needed. During the 1970s and 1980s, a number of blockbuster products came to the market which transformed the companies who discovered them. Continued profit growth following the success of a blockbuster product poses a major challenge for the future, since more and more compounds are required to sustain the same rate of growth, from R&D alone.

A greater spend in terms of the percentage of sales may be allocated for periods when a company has a number of compounds in Phase 3 development. In 1998, the top 10 companies spent over $1 billion on R&D (Table 2.1).

Table 2.1.
Company Expenditures in Research and Development

Company	Estimated 1998 Expenditures ($ billion)	Percent of Sales
Aventis*	3.00	12.5
Novartis AG	2.63	11.3
Pfizer Inc.	2.2	16.6
Glaxo Wellcome plc	1.99	14.8
AstraZeneca	1.90	11.9
Merck & Co. Inc.	1.84	6.9
Eli Lilly and Co.	1.76	17.5
American Home Products	1.54	10.9
Pharmacia & Upjohn Inc.	1.16	17.5
Schering-Plough Corp.	1.02	12.6
Total	19.07	

*Combination of HMR and RPR figures; this may be reduced in the future as synergies from the merger are realised.

Source: *Pharma Business* Jan/Feb 1999

The Research Portfolio

It is research that primes the pump for the pipeline; without an excellent research base, a steady flow of new products cannot be achieved. The areas of research in which a company engages will depend on business strategy and the expertise of the research staff. The cost of research is relatively low compared with the cost of development. Research should be sized, on average, to be capable of producing many more compounds than a company can afford to develop. Typically, large companies spend between 25 and 30 percent of their total R&D budget on drug discovery.

It is possible to calculate the size of the research effort to provide the required flow of NCEs to the market, i.e., 4 per year, 2 per year and so on. Team sizes for medicinal research chemists are optimal between 6 and 12. Some companies have larger teams, but there is debate about the efficiency with which these larger teams work. The incremental return in terms of additional compounds produced is considered to be disproportionate to the increase in headcount.

The way research is conducted is beyond the scope of this book and is much debated, with different approaches being adopted by different companies. What is important, however, is that the strategy and funding of the research effort is compatible with the strategy and funding of the development effort, if an optimal flow of new products to the market is to be sustained in the long term.

The number of teams required would depend on the number of therapeutic areas of interest to the company and the desired number of NCE launches per year. Each team of chemists requires support from biologists, and the size of these teams depends on the models and screens used. In the past, the ratio of biologists to chemists has typically been approximately 2 to 1; however, with modern techniques, this ratio can be as low as 1.2 to 1 or 1.0 to 1. In addition to these core research teams, support will be required from physical chemistry and other departments/groups; these departments can be sized according to the projected flow of compounds from the chemists.

Compounds come out of discovery at different rates; often there will be clusters followed by a dearth of suitable compounds. It is important that these situations be well managed, including the use of inward and outward licensing, co-development and other strategic alliances.

The Development Portfolio

Management of the development portfolio is much more complex, necessitating the right balance between the number of compounds being developed, the speed of progress of compounds and the probability of success in terms of (a) obtaining a marketing authorisation and (b) competitive position or potential to realise sufficient sales revenue to justify their development costs.

Resource management is much more demanding with respect to the development portfolio than with respect to the research portfolio, mainly due to the expense involved in long-term toxicology and clinical programmes and the attrition rate of compounds. On average, one New Drug Application (NDA) submission is achieved from 10 Investigational New Drug (IND) candidates, and only one IND is achieved for every three candidates nominated into exploratory development.

The development budget is largely dictated by the number of compounds in Phase 3 and the strategy determining how much work is done during Phase 2. Phase 3 clinical programmes can be extremely expensive. The central nervous system can be a particularly expensive area in which to undertake clinical programmes, and certain indications are more costly than others. For example, stroke is more difficult and expensive than epilepsy because clinical endpoints are more difficult to define, and suitable patient populations more difficult to identify or access.

Traditionally, Phase 2 clinical programmes were concerned with determining the efficacy and dose required. Even then, dose ranging and dose regimen studies were often perfunctory. In the interests of eliminating compounds which may be efficacious in absolute terms but which may not have a sufficient competitive advantage to meet sales targets when launched, more companies are spending more in Phase 2. More careful profiling is being done, which is resulting in a shift in expenditures toward Phase 2. Such strategies are cost-effective in the longer term by reducing the number of compounds which get to market, but generate sales revenues that do not justify their development and promotional costs.

The determination of the development budget requires systems to be in place to select the best project options from those available and then to determine the resources (headcount, facilities and revenue expenses) required to run the projects. The process is an iterative one, since the speed at which projects can be implemented depends on the funds being available to undertake parallel activities and for sequential activities to proceed without delays. It is not unusual for some projects to be expedited as quickly as possible and others to be taken more slowly until a critical decision point is reached and the acceptance criteria met.

Product Support

The return on investment in NCEs can be maximised by developing line extensions. New presentations, delivery systems or packaging can extend product life cycles. Reducing the cost of goods through the introduction of new manufacturing processes and new technology can increase profitability.

Line extensions may require a full development programme, including preclinical and clinical programmes, or in some cases only product design and development, bioequivalence and stability studies. Clearly, resources expended on the development of line extensions reduces those available for NCE development, but the probability of success is much higher.

Product support is not always the responsibility of R&D; many companies give the responsibility for Phase 4 clinical programmes and publications to the affiliates or to the Marketing Department. Responsibility for manufacturing cost reductions, capacity expansions and some line extensions is often given to the Technical Operations Department or an industrialisation function with Technical Operations. However, some ongoing support from R&D is inevitable, particularly in the areas of toxicology and regulatory affairs.

In summary, the management of the R&D budget requires consideration of research spending, development spending and product support spending. Management of the research portfolio requires a different approach than that of the development and product support portfolio. Management of the development portfolio is concerned mainly with risk management and resource management. For the remainder of this chapter, consideration will be given to those tools and techniques that can be applied to the development and product support portfolio. Management of the R&D portfolio is critical to the future success of companies. Demonstrating to financial analysts that the portfolio can support profit growth is crucially important to the way a pharmaceutical company is viewed by stock markets and, hence, how the share price performs.

COMMERCIAL OUTLOOK

Scientific opportunities need to be assessed in terms of the commercial outlook or potential return. A number of factors will influence the potential:

- *Environment:* Regulatory trends, healthcare policies and funding, social trends and so on.
- *Market potential:* Epidemiology of disease, prescribing trends.
- *Competition:* Competitive advantage of compound, health economic data, degree of unmet clinical need, development status of competitor products.
- *Pricing:* Pricing is a challenge in today's environment. While the United States is still an open market from a pricing perspective, Europe is becoming more and more price sensitive. The European Union has yet to achieve price harmony among its member countries. Traditionally, low-price countries such as Belgium, Spain and Italy are affecting prices granted by authorities in countries such as France and Germany. Companies must develop pricing strategies, which allow a sufficient profit margin to recoup development costs. It may be necessary not to accept prices that are too low in some countries in order to obtain competitive prices in others. Clearly, this will result in not launching some products in certain markets in the interest of long-term profitability.

An understanding of the commercial outlook is an essential element in the management of development projects. The expected annual revenues from a new product can be calculated simply as a function of the expected number of units sold and the price per unit. However, there are so many factors which impact on these functions that forecasting is very difficult for many potential new products.

The number of prescriptions expected is dependent on the efficacy and safety profile of the compound, epidemiology of the disease, healthcare policies and funding. It is important that the target profile and the minimum acceptable profile for a compound are reflected appropriately in the assessment of both potential sales volume and price, as shortfalls in meeting the target profile will affect both.

Competitor activity will impact on potential market share, directly by product competition and indirectly by competitor promotional activity and, to some extent, on the prescribing habits of opinion leaders. The ability to define a clear competitive advantage for a new product (unless it is targeted for an area of unmet need) is essential; the failure to do so may result in a new product which fails to repay its development and promotional costs.

3

Programme Management Defined

Programme management in pharmaceutical research and development (R&D) is a major management task for the senior team. The mainstream R&D processes are all project based and, by the very nature of the business, are highly complex. This complexity arises from a number of factors:

- Scientific challenges involved in drug discovery and development
- Attrition rate of projects
- Lengthy discovery and development time-scales
- Impact of competition
- Evolving regulatory requirements

This complexity must be taken into account by the programme management system for optimal decision making.

In concept, programme management is the process whereby projects are raised, evaluated, approved, funded and implemented. Project evaluation is the process by which the investment/return analysis of a project is made. It is of fundamental importance because if the sales potential of the compound does not represent a good return on investment costs, then the project should not be undertaken.

If managed properly, programme management is a process whereby for a given activity level R&D costs can be minimised; conversely, for a given development spend, a higher return in terms of future sales can be obtained. This process has two areas of focus:

1. Making the connection between business objectives and the project portfolio
2. Providing a mechanism to manage multiple projects

A programme can be defined as a portfolio of related projects undertaken in order to achieve wider business objective. These projects can be interdependent in one or more of the following ways:

- *Resource dependencies:* A limited pool of specialist resources is required for a number of different projects; hence, these projects cannot be managed separately.
- *Objective dependencies:* The achievement of the business goals depends on the outcome of more than one project.
- *Logic dependencies:* There are dependencies at the project level (e.g., line extensions will use toxicology data generated on the New Chemical Entity [NCE]).

All R&D projects are funded from a single budget. No one project can be managed in isolation, since all allocations of funds have an associated opportunity cost. The role of R&D management is to maximise the value of the R&D pipeline for a given spend. Also, within a specialty such as a therapeutic area or scientific function, skills and expertise are limited and cannot in some cases be increased immediately by using contract staff or external research facilities. This limits the number of projects that can be worked on at the same time.

Many businesses have learned that concentration on core competencies is a reliable way to maximise profitability. The pharmaceutical industry is no exception, and many companies are or have re-evaluated their areas of core competence over the last decade or so. Identification of core competencies is usually made on a therapeutic area basis. A range of compounds able to treat a wide range of indications within the therapeutic area is required for an acceptable level of profitability to be achieved.

Business objectives may require a minimum number of successful compounds to qualify a particular therapeutic area as a core competence. The failure of certain projects may, in fact, result in a re-evaluation of this particular aspect of the strategy. There has been a focus away from certain therapeutic areas as the result of the failure of products to meet forecast sales potential and a termination of key development projects as a result of the failure to meet the target product profile during development. Such a decision can result in the restructuring of sales forces and have implications for manufacturing facilities as well as the impact on R&D teams.

In development, there are also many instances of interproject dependencies, for example,

- Strategies in a given therapeutic area may seek to develop a range of related treatments. In asthma, for instance, reliever and preventor products are required.
- Line extensions for new indications or dosage forms rely on preclinical data from the NCE project.
- The process chemistry for a class of compounds will have common steps in the synthesis; therefore, process development and optimisation will also have interproject dependencies.

The success of a programme is not guaranteed by the successful completion of individual projects alone; it is dependent on the integration of project deliverables into a wider context. For the pharmaceutical industry, this wider context is maximising business growth for a given R&D spend.

THE R&D PIPELINE

A good pipeline should provide a flow of new products to the market such that revenue streams provide steady growth. As products come to the end of patent life, revenues will be reduced due to generic competition; therefore, the new product introductions must compensate for the reduction of sales from the current product range, as well as provide growth of the business as a whole. This is one aspect of the business which is driving the tendency of large companies to merge. The financial markets expect continued profit growth, and companies such as Glaxo, Hoechst Marion Rousell and so on would need to launch more new products per year than their R&D pipelines can sustain to meet the financial market expectations.

A good pipeline will have the following characteristics:

- Contain compounds in all phases of development, including filed New Drug Applications (NDAs) awaiting approval, in at least four different therapeutic areas.
- Contain a number of blockbuster drugs (having projected peak sales of at least $500 million). A blockbuster drug is most likely to be a "first in class" compound to treat life-threatening diseases in an area of relatively unmet need.
- All compounds should provide clear advantages over existing therapies.

Management of the pipeline (Figure 3.1) requires that projects be nominated and progressed (accelerated, slowed or terminated) according to the merits of the compounds and the business needs within the commercial environment.

Figure 3.1. The R&D Pipeline

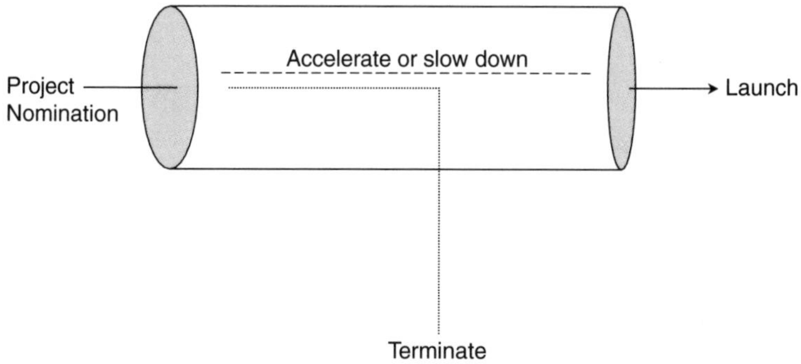

THE R&D LIFE CYCLE

Figures 3.2 and 3.3 illustrate the phases of R&D. In Figure 3.2, the development phase is illustrated by the critical aspects of the clinical programme as defined by the traditional Phases 1 to 4. In Figure 3.3, the clinical development programme is divided into proof of concept and regulatory development. This later approach is being adopted more and more in order to decrease

Figure 3.2. The R&D Life Cycle—Traditional

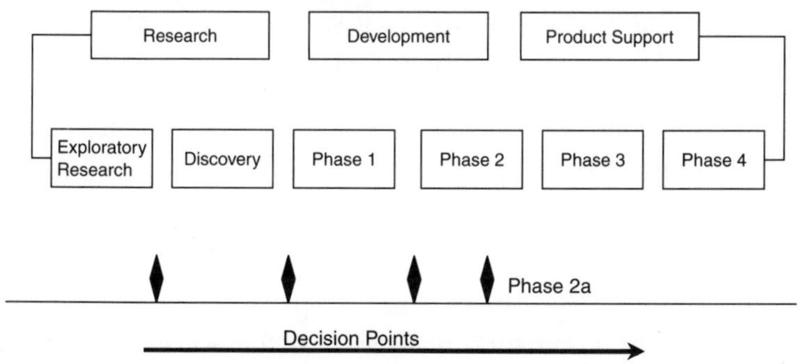

Figure 3.3. The R&D Life Cycle—Current

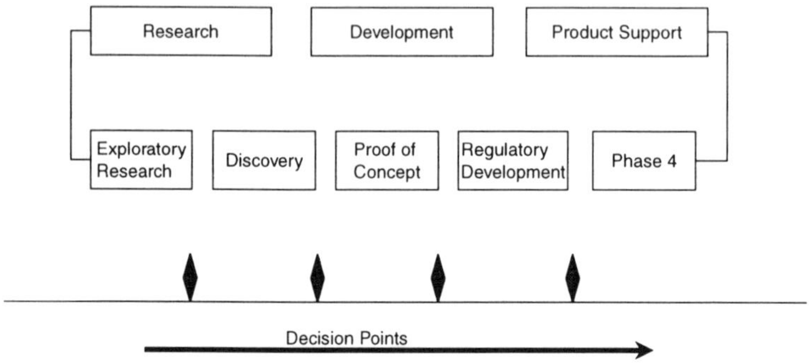

development times. The most critical aspects in the clinical development programme are establishment of the correct dose and competitive advantage.

THE BENEFITS OF A PROGRAMME MANAGEMENT APPROACH

There are a number of benefits to be gained by taking a programme management approach, providing that it becomes integrated into the ways of working for the organisation and is embraced by the senior management team in R&D and the Marketing Department. These benefits include the following:

- Revenue streams from a potential project spend can be maximised.
- Increased productivity from the Development Department will be obtained by eliminating projects that will not provide a good return on investment and from the timely termination of projects if the acceptance criteria are not met at the various project decision points.

- The quality of information on projects and the timeliness with which it becomes available is critical to good decision making. As development projects progress from Phases 1 to 3, the cost of changing, either strategy or plans, increases. Any delay in the consideration of critical information and decision making will inevitably lead to higher resource usage and other costs.

- Resource management provides a mechanism for the control of the headcount aspect of project benefits and costs.

- The development of a resource usage database and generic project plans provides a sound basis for continuous improvement in project planning, resource management and project costing for the future.

- Programme management provides a mechanism for risk management, for individual projects and for the project portfolio as a whole.

- The existence of a formal mechanism for managing projects that have interdependencies will reduce delays in communications between different project teams and, therefore, speed up decision making.

Programme management systems can be employed to support the following business activities:

- Strategic planning

- Portfolio management

- Management information

- Progress reporting

4

Portfolio Management

Research and development (R&D) are very different business activities and should not be managed in identical ways. Research costs are generally lower than those for development, but the science is more challenging. Regulatory development requires essentially the same type of activities to be undertaken for each project, can be readily planned and lends itself to the disciplines of portfolio and project management. For these reasons, only the development portfolio will be considered here.

DEVELOPMENT PORTFOLIO EVALUATION

The purpose of portfolio evaluation is to maximise the effectiveness of resource utilisation within the organisation, whilst at the same time maximising the future potential revenue streams for the business. An analysis of all project opportunities with respect to their market potential, development time-scales, resource demands and all associated risks enables projects to be eliminated if they do not fit with business objectives.

The portfolio evaluation is also the vehicle by which rational choices can be made between alternative projects or portfolios. It is important that managers and project team members understand the reasons behind project selection or cancellation if commitment to the chosen portfolio is to be obtained at all levels.

How many times have the resurrection specialists been observed at work following the cancellation of a project? This will happen if a rigourous process of evaluation and selection is not undertaken to enable good decisions to be made and if the reasons for the selections and rejections are not well communicated to all staff concerned. The consequences of these selections must also be understood and supported by the senior R&D team and commercial managers, since all resource allocations have opportunity costs, and it is not possible to please every business player all of the time.

The portfolio evaluation process (Figure 4.1) is one that involves an assessment of the commercial value of all potential projects and their probability of success. This risk-benefit analysis is then used to eliminate non-viable projects and to prioritise

Figure 4.1. The Portfolio Evaluation Process

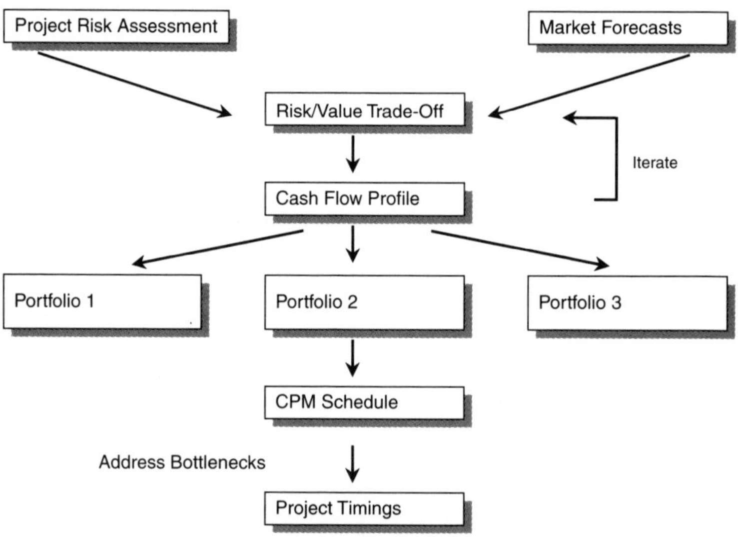

projects for resource allocation. If insufficient resources are available to fund all potential projects, choices have to be made. Making choices between projects requires knowledge of the medium- and long-term business objectives as well as the merits of individual projects.

What Is the Right Balance in a Development Portfolio?

The right balance is really about the management of risk, the most significant ones being the potential of a compound to receive a marketing authorisation, which is largely dependent on safety and efficacy, and realisation of sales revenue. Sales are dependent on a number of factors, including competitive advantage of the compound and its presentation, launch timing, promotional budget and pricing.

New Chemical Entities (NCEs) have a higher risk than do line extensions, but the sales revenues associated with line extensions are often lower than for NCEs. However, bearing in mind that some new compounds never recoup their development costs, line extensions can play a very valuable role in a portfolio, particularly for smaller companies.

NCEs fall into a number of categories that will impact on the safety and efficacy risk and also on their potential revenues:

- Novel candidates in an established class
- Me-too candidates in an established class
- Early entrants in a new class
- Late entrants in a new class

It is more difficult to make a commercial success of me-too candidates in an established class than for a truly novel candidate. For these compounds, a clear competitive advantage, e.g., economics of treatment and so on, should be established. Daily dosing and pricing may well be crucial to their success. Similarly, early entrants in a new class are likely to have a significant advantage, and speed to market to maintain competitive advantage is critical.

There is no right answer as to the correct balance (Figure 4.2); it depends on the company's business strategy, the approach to risk in the development portfolio and the opportunities afforded by the compounds available. However, understanding the nature of the risks involved and building appropriate decision criteria into reviews of the development portfolio are keys to maximising the rate of return on the investment in product development.

Risk Management

The majority of compounds nominated for development do not reach the market. This high attrition rate is merely a reflection of the high degree of risk in the process of drug development; however, if this risk is not well managed, the cost of development will be higher than necessary. Another way of looking at the cost of risk is that for a given activity level where risk in the development portfolio is well managed development costs will be lower.

Figure 4.3 shows two portfolios with approximately equal average values or potential revenue streams. However, portfolio 1 has a lower risk in that the range of possible revenues is

Figure 4.2. Inputs and Outputs to the Portfolio Evaluation Process

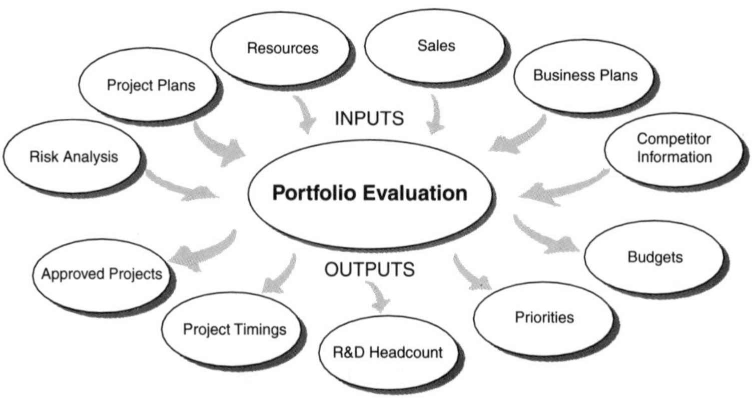

Figure 4.3. The Nature of Risk

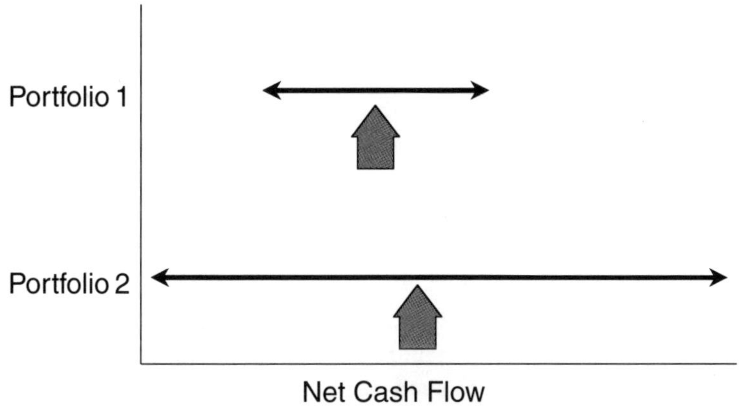

smaller. Portfolio 2 contains some potential as a blockbuster, but there is a significant risk that none of the projects will produce valuable marketed products. The revenue streams range from very low to very high.

Spreading the Risks

Consideration should be given to the following types of risk:

- Projects with different scientific risks
- Projects with different commercial risks
- Different stages in development
- Different markets and sizes
- Consideration of emerging markets

Quantification of Risk

There is no absolute way of quantifying risk, but for portfolio management, all that is really required is to understand the categories of risk, i.e., high, medium and low, and to understand the relative risk between projects competing for the same resources. It is also necessary to understand the relationship between the risk involved in a chosen portfolio and the potential return. This risk-return analysis (Figure 4.4) can be used to eliminate projects that do not fit with the business strategy, it can also be used on a project-by-project basis in order to choose between projects in terms of resource allocation or prioritisation.

Projects in the high risk/low return category are not desirable in the portfolio; however, an understanding of what factors place them in this category is the key element. It may be that the assessment of low return is due to poor strategic fit or the ability to get the compound to market before the competition, hence eroding potential market share. In such cases, outlicensing the compound or forming an alliance to co-develop or co-market the product may be appropriate.

Most NCEs will fall into the high risk/high return category in the early phase of development. The risk reduces as each decision point in the project plan is reached. By the end of Phase 3, the scientific risk may be low, but more will be known about other risk

Figure 4.4. Risk-Return Analysis, Part 1

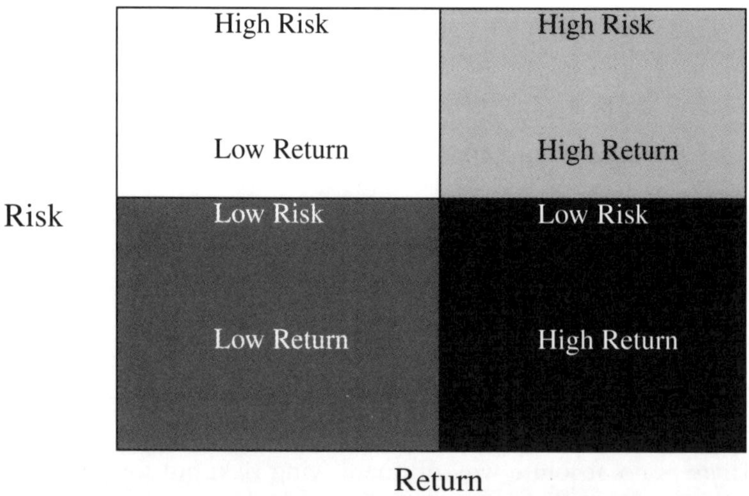

factors, such as competition and the likelihood of achieving the target profile. Sales forecasts will become more precise as first launches approach.

Line extensions can fall into the low risk/low return category or low risk/high return category depending on the nature of the compound being developed. Line extensions in the low risk/low return category are often worth pursuing, particularly if the current portfolio has few products in Phase 3, where the risk is lower than for Phases 1 and 2.

Line extensions are a good way of spreading the risk in a portfolio and maximising the return on investment previously made in an NCE. Good line extensions can prolong the life cycle of products for a significant period of time, and new delivery systems can provide a barrier to entry by generic competition.

In the area of respiratory diseases, this can be particularly valuable. New devices have a marked competitive advantage over compounds, which of themselves do not have a marked advantage.

Many companies are including developing or emerging markets in their business strategies. Here consideration should be given to the cost of the product and where the product will be manufactured. Sophisticated but very expensive presentations may not be appropriate for these markets, and projects aimed at reducing manufacturing and packaging costs for products destined for these markets may well have a place in a product support portfolio.

One of the most frequently used methods to evaluate risk is to identify each of the various elements that comprise the overall risk and score each one. Return can be assessed in the same way by scoring or by using actual sales forecasts. If actual sales forecasts are preferred, it is necessary to calculate NPV (net present value) in order to correct for the time-scale over which the revenues are expected.

Given the volatile nature of sales forecasts for products in the early stages of development, single-point forecasts can be very misleading. The sensitivity of sales to the achievement of the target profile must be understood, therefore, it is sensible to establish forecasts for the scenario where all parameters of the target profile are met and for the scenario where only the minimum acceptable profile is met. The differences can in some cases be very significant. The scoring method for sales is a useful tool for a rough-cut portfolio assessment or for prioritising projects where there is a severe resource conflict.

DETERMINATION OF RISK IN A DEVELOPMENT PROJECT PORTFOLIO

Given below is a simple method for determining risk in a development portfolio. It involves the identification of components of risk, which are then scored by a number of individuals. These scores are then weighted for respondents (more explanation will be provided as the example is worked through) and normalised to provide a set of scores that can be plotted against return.

Components of Risk

The first step is to identify the components of risk. Given below are some categories that have been used in my experience, but other categories may be appropriate according to the organisation and its specific needs.

Strategic Need

Strategic need is an assessment of the degree of fit to the business strategy and core competencies of the business. Compounds that fit the highest priority of the business strategy are most likely to provide higher revenues. If a compound is a poor fit, the company will not have the resources to fully maximise the opportunity, either in development because expertise may be lacking or in marketing. Poor fit with the marketed product range will reduce sales or will require higher costs to achieve the sales potential.

If the market potential of a new compound is so high as to make it a likely blockbuster, then the sales potential should compensate for a lack of certain expertise. The shortfalls must be recognised, and appropriate action taken to close the gap. The benefit of the analysis is to make the senior team aware of strengths and weaknesses and to encourage the development of appropriate strategies and plans.

Sensitivity

The sensitivity of the sales forecasts should be evaluated. This should include an assessment of the competition, the sensitivity of the forecasts to the achievement of the target profile and so on. Achievement of the minimum acceptable profile rather than the target profile could have significant impact upon potential revenues.

Clinical

There should be a clinical evaluation of the risk of the compound. The clinical evaluation will determine if the compound meets the acceptance criteria given in the target profile for clinical safety, efficacy, dose regimen and any comparative parametric requirements.

Preclinical/Toxicology

The preclinical/toxicology evaluation will determine if the compound will meet the safety criteria defined in the target profile.

Pharmaceutical

Pharmaceutical risk is an assessment that the desired dosage form cannot be developed in an acceptable time-scale and/or the cost of goods will not be achieved by the required time after launch. (Three years is a good rule of thumb.) Areas where pharmaceutical risk may be high include the development of controlled-release formulations and novel drug delivery systems, including nasal delivery and patches. Specialist or novel delivery systems include dry powder devices for dose delivery to the lung for respiratory disorders. Regulatory requirements, particularly in the United States for dose uniformity, are extremely challenging for device design and manufacture.

Marketing Fit

Account should be taken of the core competencies of the Marketing Department and the fit of the product to the rest of the product range. The lack of a good fit will attenuate potential sales due to lack of either skills or experience or just numbers in the sales force. For example, a sales force that is experienced in selling to general practitioners may not be best able to exploit a hospital use product.

Project Champion

If a project has a high profile and an influential champion in either R&D or Marketing, it is more likely to progress than if such a champion does not exist. There are many examples of where R&D directors or chief executives have taken a personal interest in a compound, which has resulted in rapid development times being achieved. All other things being equal, a high profile project champion can have an enormous impact on the success of a project.

Competence

Competence is an assessment of the fit of the project to the core competencies of R&D and/or Marketing. Clearly, if a project requires skills that are outside these competencies, there will be a risk to the quality of work done and to the timings assumed in the project plan. The most common result of inappropriate development competencies is protracted regulatory approval times (for both Investigational New Drugs and New Drug Applications).

Scoring Projects for Risk

The illustration below is an example of a form (Table 4.1) used to collect scores against the categories described above for a number of projects. With this method of risk assessment, projects are given a score for each category from 1 to 10, where 1 is high and 10 is low. Individuals are asked to score each project. For a better

Table 4.1.
Project Risk Assessment Questionnaire

	Market Fit	Sensitivity	Pharmaceutical Risk	Toxicology Risk	Clinical Risk	Competence	Project Champion	Strategic Need
Project 1								
Project 2								
Project 3								
Project 4								
Project 5								
Project 6								
Project 7								
Project 8								
Project 9								
Project 10								
Project 11								
Project 12								
Project 13								
Project 14								
Project 15								

outcome, a number of different individuals should be included from the following departments:

- Pharmacology
- Toxicology
- Clinical Pharmacology
- Clinical Research
- Pharmaceutical Sciences
- Regulatory Affairs
- Technical Operations/Industrialisation
- Marketing
- Project Direction

Each member of the evaluation panel should be asked to score against each risk category. When the data are analysed, the responses should be weighted such that the expert opinion makes the most significant contribution. In some cases, individuals will not feel qualified to assess certain categories and will not do so. However, this approach can be extremely beneficial since the medical staff will have a very good experience base to comment on the marketing risk (a clinical trial is an excellent test marketing exercise) and preclinical risk as do regulatory staff. Operations will have a good experience base for pharmaceutical risk and so on.

The individuals involved in the risk assessment must be sufficiently senior to understand the implications of the scoring. For this reason, either the core project team members or their department managers (if these are not the same) should be involved. A good check on the scoring is to have the appropriate function heads review their scores with the team before they are submitted for analysis. This step is useful because if projects are ultimately eliminated from the portfolio, there will be some individuals who will question the analysis if their pet project does not make the approved project list.

Gaining commitment at each stage of the portfolio analysis from the key members of the management team is important if the outcome is to be accepted.

ANALYSIS OF RISK IN THE DEVELOPMENT PORTFOLIO

Upon completion of the questionnaires, the scores should be weighted, normalised and summed. These scores are then plotted against the forecast return. The return can be estimated simply in millions of dollars, or the NPV for each product can be calculated. The NPV will clearly take into account the time for which the revenues can be expected, but use of the NPV in a mix of projects in different phases of development, e.g., line extensions and NCEs, can produce distortion in favour of short-term product launches with smaller returns. Under these circumstances, it may be better to do two separate analyses, one for short-term launches (e.g., for the next three years) and one for longer-term launches (e.g., three to six years).

Risk-Return Analysis

Figure 4.5 contains all the projects that have been evaluated. Clearly, the most desirable projects will be in the high return/low risk category. However, most NCEs will be in the high risk category unless they are close to launch, since risks reduce as compounds progress. Line extensions will generally be in the lower risk areas but will have lower returns associated with them.

High risk/low return projects should be eliminated from the portfolio early in the process. If resources are not available to fund every project remaining after any high risk/low return projects have been eliminated, different scenarios can be developed by constructing different portfolios with different risk return profiles, then choices can be made according to the business strategy.

From an understanding of the components of risk, it is possible to take action to reduce or to spread out the risk. If, for

Figure 4.5. Risk-Return Analysis, Part 2

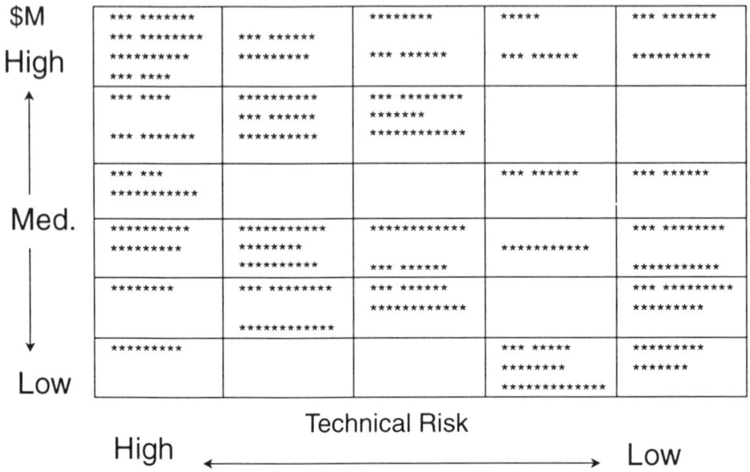

instance, for a given project the competence element of the risk is high because a compound does not fit the core competencies, a development partner can be sought to bring in expertise and to share in the development and promotional costs.

This analysis can be used not only to eliminate projects from the portfolio but also to prioritise them for resource allocation. If resources are limited, it may be necessary to progress some high risk projects more slowly, by not running parallel programmes, until certain decision points are reached. As each decision point is reached, some of the elements of risk (clinical, preclinical and pharmaceutical) will be reduced, making the project more attractive with respect to resource allocation.

From the risk-return analysis, a number of different portfolios can be analysed and evaluated for their potential to meet the business needs. The timing of new product introductions along with their associated revenue streams should be considered against the strategic business objectives for sales and profit growth in order to select one that meets the overall business strategy. For instance, if patents for one or more existing marketed products are to expire over the short term, the desired portfolio is one which introduces new products at about the same time as the patents expire. If, however, this is not an issue for the short term, because sufficient products are still early in their life cycles, a portfolio which produces NCEs at a time when current products are reaching their peak sales may be more appropriate.

If it is not possible to obtain the revenues required to sustain the growth targets of the company from the current portfolio, strategies need to be developed to fill the projected profit gap (Figure 4.6). A number of possibilities can be considered, including

- line extensions of existing NCEs,
- inward licences,
- co-development agreements and
- co-marketing of newly licenced products in areas of core competencies.

Figure 4.6. The Strategic Framework

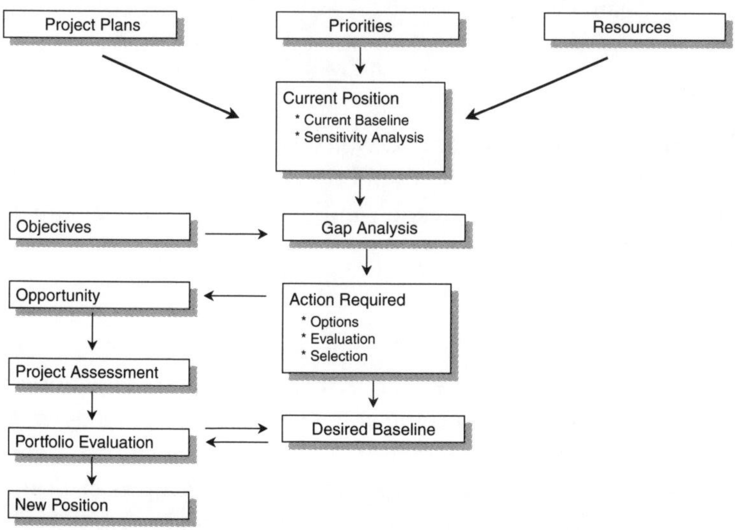

With the exception of line extentions, these options require finding suitable companies with the right compounds to fill the gaps.

Line extensions of existing NCEs are the fastest way of increasing revenues internally, either by introducing new product lines or presentations or by increasing the indications for currently marketed products. Line extensions are low risk in that the toxicity of the compound is known, and there is a good knowledge of pharmacology and efficacy. However, they are unlikely to provide the level of revenue of a major NCE, so several line extensions may be required to meet profit growth targets.

Inward licences and co-development can be extremely attractive ways of filling gaps in the portfolio, providing that suitable opportunity can be found. The management of these projects, especially co-development projects, requires additional skills to those required for the management of internal projects. The following areas need careful attention:

- Clear contract definition
- Project leadership
- Project management
- Team skills

Clear Contract Definition

The contract must be clear and well communicated to the project team. Ideally, the contract should define how the project will be managed, with roles and responsibilities for each party adequately defined.

Project Leadership

Different companies have different cultures and development philosophies, ways of working and styles in project management and communication. Project teams have to be able to function successfully in all cultures. Appropriate leadership is critical to the success. The project leader needs to be a senior, experienced individual who can integrate best practices and create a cohesive, well-motivated team.

Project Management

Progress needs to be monitored and communicated appropriately. The timely resolution of technical issues is more difficult to achieve because communications are complicated when team members are at different geographical locations. If these distances are great time differences, for example, between the United States and Europe or Asia, the window for telephone conversations is reduced to just a few hours a day. The use of email, voice mail, PicTel and video conferences will help communications, but strong team relationships can only built with face-to-face contact. A steering group, with appropriate representation from both companies is a good way of providing support to the project team.

Team Skills

Project team members can benefit from some training in cross-company working, taking into account the nationalities of the team members. (This is also important within large international companies.) A co-development project with a Japanese company, for example, will expose some team members to different philosophies and ways of working for the first time.

There are some fundamental differences between the operational methods of a European company and an American company. Even within Europe there are differences, for example, within French companies, agreements reached in project team meetings will be discussed further with co-workers outside the meeting, and what was thought to have been agreed may change afterward with further input and discussion.

Americans tend to negotiate very hard and push their views strongly at meetings, often believing that a certain course of action has been agreed on because no one disagreed. When events unfold differently, frustration can cause strained relationships. These issues will be discussed further in Chapter 11.

5

Resource Management

One of the most expensive resources is headcount (others being external research and drug substance costs), and Development managers need to control this aspect carefully. Effective headcount management requires a good understanding of the resources available for development projects. Although this statement seems obvious, it is my experience that managers overestimate the actual time available for projects because they underestimate the amount of effort required for essential support activities. Non-essential support activities are often not managed by the senior team. Decisions are taken at the supervisor level, and the impact on the development projects is never understood.

Clearly, the senior team cannot get involved with approving or other specific support tasks, but it is possible to manage the amount of time allocated to specific categories of activity, the details of which can be managed by the department manager or at the supervisor level. The ratio of direct project workers to indirect project workers (non-project workers or support staff) and the various categories of work to which they are routinely allocated are described below.

WORK CATEGORIES

Direct project workers are involved with the following work categories:

- Research
- Development
- Product support
- Method and systems development and support
- Project management
- Management and supervision
- Training and development

Research and Development

Research and development (R&D) includes all projects specified in the R&D portfolios and are all contained on the project list. Development projects will include New Chemical Entities (NCEs) and line extension projects.

Product Support

Product support can include some or all of the following:

- Phase 4 programmes—these projects will usually be on the official project list
- Pharmacovigilance–marketed products
- Complaint investigations
- Competitor product analysis
- Bioequivalence studies—may or may not be on the project list (support for site changes handled by operations may not be included)

- Clinical or toxicology studies for process or material changes
- Stability studies
- New regulatory submissions and licence updates for marketed products
- Process and test method improvements
- Troubleshooting for process and test methods

Methods and Systems Development

Improvements in ways of working is an ongoing activity for all departments. Such systems will include the following:

- Analytical methodologies
- Laboratory information management systems (LIMSs)
- Database system development
- Clinical trial management systems
- Project management and planning methodologies
- New technology research and evaluation

Management and Supervision

Management and supervision are activities required to manage departments and teams, including people development, objective setting, management of budgets, facilities management, staff meetings and so on. This category can also include those activities required to manage projects within project management functions and within line functions.

Training and Development

Training and development involves allocating time to attend conferences and seminars, preparing publications, part-time formal education and so on.

Indirect or Support Staff

Support staff are workers who do not work on projects directly. They are involved with a range of support services, including the following:

- Secretarial and administrative
- Engineering and maintenance
- Human resources
- Finance
- Information systems
- Purchasing and stores
- Security and cleaning

Analysis of Work Categories

A more detailed breakdown of work categories and responsibilities is given in Table 5.1. A rough-cut analysis of the proportion of the R&D headcount spent on these categories can be obtained by providing department managers with a questionnaire to complete over a short period of time. Four weeks should be sufficient if formal time recording systems are not in place.

Formal time recording systems of some kind are in operation within most companies for development projects for accounting purposes, but such systems are often not in place for research and support staff. Time recording will be discussed further since a major application is to support project planning and headcount planning for the budget.

Table 5.1.
Research and Development Work Categorisation

Holidays and Sickness	Public	
	Annual entitlement	
	Sickness	
Development and Training	Formal education	Masters and PhD
	Knowledge and skills	Conferences and seminars
		Secondments
Management and Supervision	Line management	People development
		Budgets
		Direction
		Facilities
	Project management	Project leadership
		Planning
Method and Systems Support	R&D methodology	Model development
		Screen development
	Systems development	LIMS
		Document management
		Clinical trials data capture and reporting systems
Support Services	Administrative	Secretarial, typing documentation and archiving
		Travel
	Engineering and Maintenance	New facilities
		Services: Plant and equipment
		Maintenance planned and breakdown
	Human resources	Selection, development
		Remuneration
	Finance	Budgets
	Information systems	Systems development and existing system support
	Purchasing	Contracts: Ordering and stores

Table 5.1 continued on the next page

Table 5.1 continued from the previous page

Product Support—Non-Project	Regulatory	Product licence maintenance
	Market support	Competitor product analysis
		Complaints
	Plant and process support	Bioequivalence testing
		Troubleshooting
Development Projects	NCE development	From own research
		Co-development
		Inward licence
	Line extensions	Reformulation
		New delivery systems
		New indications
		New dosage strengths
	Product support projects	Phase 4 programmes
		Publications
		Capacity expansion
		Pack development
Research Projects	NCE discovery	

Having undertaken an exercise of work category analysis in the past, I was surprised to discover what a small proportion of the total headcount was available to spend on the development of NCEs. I have since learned that this is true of many companies—the time spent on product support, line extensions and methods and systems development (including supporting and maintaining laboratory equipment and computers) is very significant.

All of these activities are important and need to be resourced; however, if the value from R&D is to be maximised, it is important that the management team understand how resources are being allocated. Product support and methods support activities can be particularly important in the management of peaks and troughs in development project workload.

Work categorisation is only important from a management perspective in understanding how time is spent and how the current allocation fits with business strategies. If the business strategy is to launch a certain number of NCEs per year, then the allocation of resources between the categories in Table 5.1 must fit with the strategy. It is my experience that managers do not really understand the actual allocation of time at the project worker level. If there is not a management mechanism in place, he or she who shouts loudest tends to get the resources.

There is no right answer to the question, "How much time should be allocated to each work category?" It is important that the management team understand and approve the overall percentage of time spent on each category. What is most important is the definition and approval of time available for development projects, which will be used in the portfolio review. In my experience, the time available for development projects is approximately 20–25 percent of the total R&D headcount.

An approximate analysis of typical resource usage is given in Table 5.2. This will vary greatly from company to company, and the only purpose of including such an analysis here is to provoke an enquiry as to what is appropriate and how work category analysis can help a company to manage resources.

Table 5.2.
Typical Work Category Analysis

Activity	% Total Time Utilised
Research projects	10–15
Development projects	25–30
Method support	04–05
Management and supervision	03–05
Non-project support activities	35–45
Training	02–03
Vacation and sickness	10–13

RESOURCE PLANNING AND MANAGEMENT FOR DEVELOPMENT PROJECTS

Resource management consists of determining how much resources are required to progress each project in the portfolio, calculating the total requirement and comparing it with available resources. Any shortfalls can be managed by delaying projects, adding additional resource or contracting out appropriate work. Figure 5.1 summarises the steps described in this section on resource management.

Project plans for each project on the approved list must be developed with resource allocations for each activity. For this purpose, the project plan does not need to be detailed to several hundred activities; a generic or standard project is suitable for resource planning.

Since the time-scales for clinical and preclinical activities vary with therapeutic area, the development of a number of generic project plans will serve as a way to assess a new project quickly. These generic plans provide a starting point for project teams when more detailed plans are required for implementation. The

Figure 5.1. Resource Management

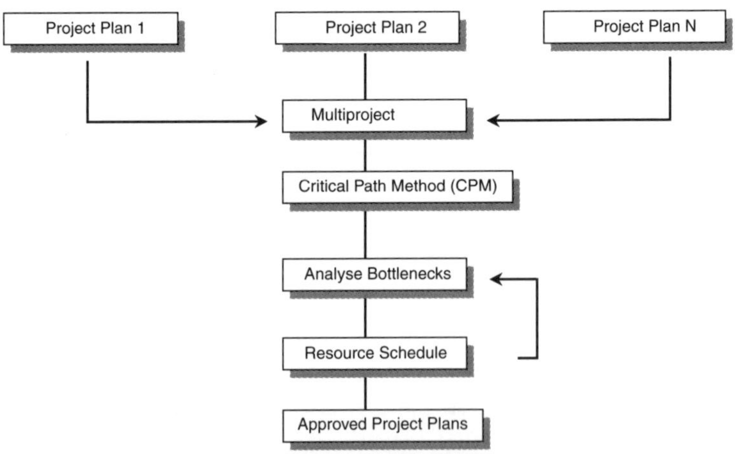

generic plans in Table 5.3 will prove extremely useful for planning purposes.

For the NCE development, a plan consisting of between approximately 100 and no more than 150 activities is sufficient for resource planning. Any further detail does not improve the accuracy and serves only to make the planning process bureaucratic.

Resource estimates should be made by skill types, where the definition of a skill is broad enough to identify the general skills required—training can always be given for very specialist skills—but should be specific enough to avoid inappropriate allocation of tasks. For example, an analytical chemist who has experience in the primary area supporting drug synthesis could be assigned to stability testing or to secondary formulation development analysis, since the same basic skills are required. However, the assignment of an analytical chemist to undertake preclinical

Table 5.3.
Generic Planning

Therapeutic Area	Type of Project
Cardiovascular	NCE development
	Line extension—new indication
	Line extention—new dosage form
Central nervous system	NCE development
	Line extension—new indication
	Line extension—new dosage form
Anti-infective	NCE development
	Line extension—new indication
	Line extension—new dosage form
Respiratory	NCE development
	Line extension—new indication
	Line extension—new dosage form
	New device development
General other	NCE development
	Line extension—new indication
	Line extension—new dosage form

toxicology work could not be achieved without a significant amount of education and training.

This allocation of resource types as opposed to the estimation of total man-years of effort enables a determination of where skill shortages are present. It may be possible to have sufficient total numbers of staff, but if the distribution of skills available does not match those required, delays in project timings will be inevitable.

Table 5.4 lists some resource types that will be useful for resource planning. The list is not exhaustive, and different companies will have different definitions, but it is sufficient to demonstrate the principle here.

In pharmaceutical sciences, the resource type formulator has not been broken down into different gallenic forms. Some companies may wish to add this additional level of detail, but, in general, pharmacists can be allocated to the development of different dosage forms with appropriate supervision. Similarly, regulatory managers have not been subdivided. Some companies allocate regulatory staff to a particular area such as chemistry, manufacturing and controls (CMC); clinical, preclinical and so on and may want to reflect this in the resource type definitions.

When a list of resource types has been agreed on, estimates of resource requirements can be allocated to each of the activities defined in the project plan. An example of a generic NCE development project is given in Chapter 2.

Man-weeks is a convenient unit of measure and should be an estimate of the work content, not elapsed time. For example, for an activity such as a process chemistry campaign for stage one toxicology, an estimate of the total duration of the activity and an estimate of the resources by resource type is required. If the estimated time is 4 months (88 working days), and there are 2 process chemists working on this activity full time (no allowance for holidays or training), then the resource estimate is 35 man-weeks. If the work can be done during the summer and both chemists can take two weeks vacation and still make the drug quantities on time, then the resource estimate is 31 man-weeks.

When plans and resource estimates are available for all projects, the total resource requirements can be calculated. The results

Table 5.4.
Resource Types by Department

Department	Resources Type
Process Chemistry	Process research chemists
	Process development chemists
Analytical Chemistry	Analytical chemists
	Stability analysts
Toxicology	Toxicologists
	Pathologists
	Histopathologists
Pharmacology	Pharmacologist—cardiovascular
	Pharmacologist—respiratory etc.
Biochemistry	Biochemists
	Drug metabologists
	Bioanalytical chemists
Pharmaceutical Sciences	Pre-formulation technologists
	Development formulators
	Process development technologists
	Packaging engineers
	Microbiologists
Clinical Trial Supplies	Manufacturers
	Packaging technicians
Quality Control	Quality control specialists
Clinical Pharmacology	Clinicians
	Research associates
	Nurses
Therapeutic Research	Clinicians
	Research associates
	Statisticians
Regulatory Affairs	Regulatory managers/officers

can be calculated by the critical path method or the resource smoothed method.

Project Management Software

There are many user-friendly software packages available today which will run on personal computers (PCs). The level of expertise required to use them is well within the grasp of project planners and project analysts.

Project management software has a facility for calculating the total resource requirements for a number of projects. Each project plan is kept in a single file, and a multiproject file can be created for analysis and reporting. The multiproject file can be used in two scheduling modes: the critical path method (CPM) or resource smoothed methods.

Critical Path Method

The CPM schedules projects according to the time for each activity and its associated logic links (predecessors). It takes no account of resource availability, and reports of resource requirements for the total project list can be obtained. The resource requirements can be reported for each resource type on a monthly, quarterly or yearly basis.

Total requirements for each department can also be calculated for the same time periods, providing that resource types are associated with departments. It is good practice to develop a hierarchical relationship of resource types, breaking down from R&D to individual resources types (Figure 5.2).

Resource Smoothed Method

In the resource smoothed method, the software asks for projects to be prioritised, and resources are allocated to the highest priority project first. However, this method is not suitable for resource management for a project portfolio, since the software makes very simple allocations and will not take all scenarios into account. For portfolio management purposes, project plans are usually developed in outline only, since too much detail adds a level of

Figure 5.2. The Critical Path Method

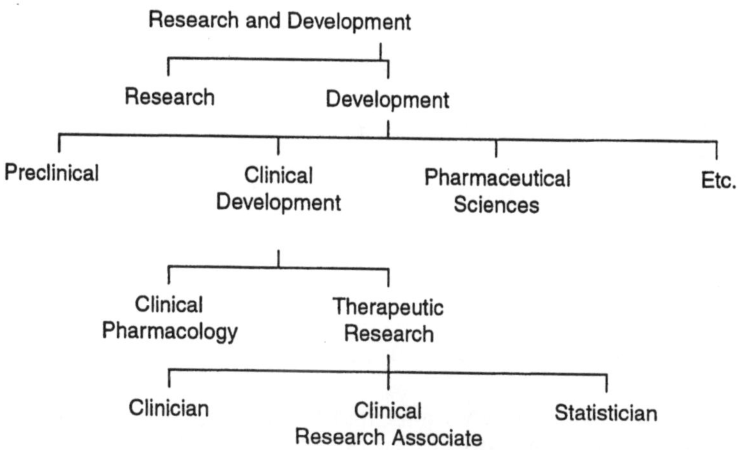

complexity which is not helpful. In many cases, standard project plans are used (developed for a specific therapeutic area). These plans are defined at a relatively high level, going down to only level three or four in the work breakdown structure. Therefore, multiple resource types will be allocated to a single activity. For example, a Phase 1 clinical pharmacology study may have clinicians, research associates and nurses allocated to it. If there is a shortfall of clinician availability, the whole activity will be delayed, and it will not be easy to understand the overall shortfall in resources.

More management information can be easily obtained by using simple reports that show the actual man-weeks of effort required in a given period. The actual resource shortfalls and overages can be readily seen, and a good understanding of all resource issues that need to be addressed is easily obtained.

Spreadsheets

For a small number of projects, the resource estimates can be entered into a spreadsheet, and the resource type and departmental totals calculated. This method does not require expertise in project management software, but is more labour intensive in the long term.

Identification and Analysis of Resource Bottlenecks

Identification of resource bottlenecks requires knowledge of requirements and availabilities. With resource requirements identified from project plans, resource availability can be calculated. This is the time available for development projects for each resource type.

Calculation of Resource Availability

The categories of all work allocated to a particular resource type must be identified. Table 5.5 is a worked example for analytical chemists. The time available can be considered as a budget, which the department manager must monitor and control. If it is agreed that 70 percent of analyst time will be allocated to development

Table 5.5.
Resource Availability for Analytical Chemists

Work Category	% Time Allocated for Analytical Chemists	% Time Allocated for Team Leaders	Total
Vacation and sickness	12	12	
Product support	05		
Methods support	10		
Laboratory support	03		
Management and supervision	00	30	
Total	30		
Time available for development projects	70	58	
Number of analysts	36		
Number of team leaders		4	
Man-weeks available for development projects	**1,310**	**120**	**1,430**

projects, the department manager must make sure that the time allocated to product support, e.g., for competitor product analysis, test method troubleshooting and so on, does not significantly exceed 5 percent. In addition, the total of product and method support should not significantly exceed 15 percent. Hence the term, work category budget (WCB) will be used to describe the time available.

The total number of man-weeks available for 36 analytical chemists is calculated as follows:

$$36 \times 0.70 \times 52 = 1{,}310 \text{ man-weeks available}$$

0.70 is the percentage time or WCB for development projects divided by 100; 52 is the total number of weeks per year. Note the work category budget has already taken vacations into account; therefore, 52 weeks is correct.

The number of man-weeks available for analytical team leaders and managers can be calculated in the same way, but the additional work category of management and supervision should be included. Therefore, the WCB for development projects for team leaders will be less than the 70 percent for analysts. In the example given in Table 5.5, the time available for development projects for team leaders can be calculated as follows:

$$4 \times 0.58 \times 52 = 120 \text{ man-weeks available}$$

The total time available for the department is, therefore, 1,430 man-weeks.

Calculating the percent utilisation for each resource type, where percent utilisation is the time required divided by the time available expressed as a percentage, can identify resource bottlenecks. Resource types whose utilisation is outside the range of 90 to 110 percent at any time during a year should be examined in more detail.

The simplest way to illustrate resource shortfalls or bottlenecks is to produce a histogram for each resource. Figures 5.3 and 5.4 illustrate two different resource bottlenecks.

Figure 5.3 shows a consistent projection of overutilisation of resources. Both the WCB availability and the 100 percent availability are below the project requirements. This means that

Figure 5.3. Resource Bottlenecks for Bioanalytical Chemists

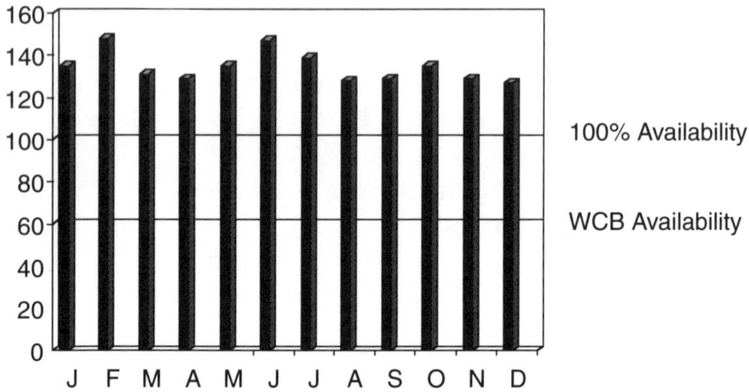

changing the WCB by delaying some method or product support activities cannot resource the development projects. In this case, some project activities must be delayed or additional resources obtained.

If project activities are delayed, the impact on major project milestones can be minimised if project activities can be identified that are not on the critical path of the specific project. Activities can be delayed until they become part of the critical path, and such scenarios can be modelled to help in the decision process.

If additional resources are added, these can be in the form of contracting out suitable activities, bringing in temporary contract resources or hiring additional permanent employees. If additional staff are recruited (temporary or permanent), then it should be noted that the WCB for these additional staff needs only to include vacation and any training, since the method support or product support activities are already resourced.

Figure 5.4 shows a different situation. The bottleneck occurs for a few months, and then resource requirements fall below the 100 percent availability and eventually fall below the WCB availability. This situation can be managed without adding resources but by choosing to delay activities.

Figure 5.4. Resource Bottlenecks for Clinical Research Associates

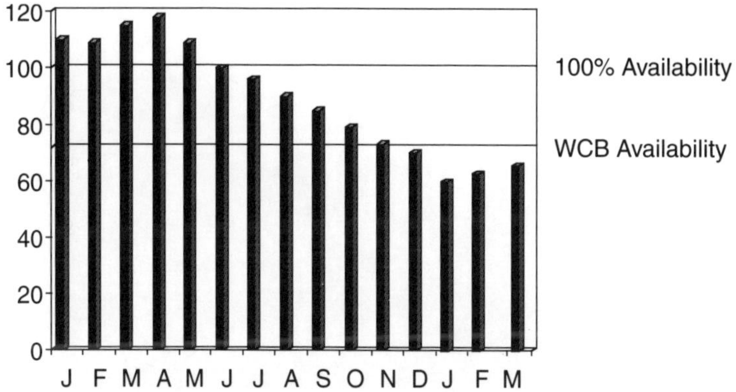

The first scenario to model in this case would be to determine the impact of delaying the non-project activities, such as product support and methods support so that the 100 percent resource availability is assumed. If this scenario is practical, the remaining shortfall can be addressed by delaying project activities, starting with non-critical path activities, to minimise the impact on the achievement of major project milestones.

It should be remembered that if there will be project decision points within the time frame for which the resource analysis is being undertaken, then it is likely that one or more projects may not progress, and, therefore, the resources may not be needed. Conversely, new project nominations may increase the requirements. Potential nominations can be included in the analysis, and a view can be taken as to the probability of projects not progressing to the next decision point. It is not necessary to undergo complex probability analysis; provision of the analysis to the function head or department manager concerned is all that is required, such that the decision can be taken in light of this individual's experience. Contingency plans can be developed if the assumptions are later proven to be inaccurate.

6

Time Recording Systems

Time recording systems are an important element of resource management. Resource estimates for future project activities are forecasts and are subject to the inaccuracies of any forecast. The accuracy of forecasting can be improved by recording the actual resource usage for a project, which will over time form a good historical basis for estimating resource requirements for similar activities.

Time recording systems can be developed in database packages such as Microsoft Access®, or off-the-shelf systems can be obtained, although most of these will not integrate readily with project management software. Simple recording systems can be developed using spreadsheets, and a pilot system can be developed easily.

FUNCTIONAL REQUIREMENTS OF AN EFFECTIVE TIME RECORDING SYSTEM

The following are the basic requirements for a time recording system:

- The system should be simple to operate.
- Data should be collected weekly.
- Discipline should be maintained, and missing timesheets should be reported.
- Department secretaries are well placed to do progress chasing.
- Data collection forms should be simple and easy to fill in.
- Direct computer entry is preferable.
- If hard-copy forms are used to collect data, then entry into the computer database is best done by department secretaries.

Fisons introduced a time recording system into research and development (R&D) in the late 1980s as part of a resource management system. The system was originally written in Oracle® but was rewritten in Microsoft Access® in the early 1990s when it was extended to the Technical Operations Department.

The database held a complete list of all project and nonproject activities for every department. Department managers selected those projects and activities for which reports were needed. R&D projects had project numbers assigned to them for other purposes, and these were also used for the timesheet system. Given below are examples of inputs to the Fisons system.

Figure 6.1 represents an activity code list for a department, which was used as a lookup table for individuals to help them select activities and associated codes when filling in their weekly timesheet. Figure 6.2 is a weekly timesheet which every individual, including managers, filled in. Department secretaries entered data when the system was first introduced; later, electronic data capture replaced the manual method.

Figure 6.1. Departmental Timesheet Code List

Department: Pharmaceutical Sciences—Inhalation Technology

Work Category	Activity Description	Code Number
Development Projects	Project 12345	12345
	Project 12367	12367
	Project 12396	12396
	Project 12329	12329
	Project 12034	12034
	Project 12563	12563
	Project 14575	14575
	Project 14523	14523
	Project 12366	12366
	Project 12452	12452
	Project 12460	12460
	Project 13425	13425
Research Projects	Project 99934	99934
	Project 99946	99946
	Project 99947	99947
Holiday and Sickness	Public holiday	00001
	Annual entitlement	00002
	Sickness	00003
Development and Training	Training	00004
	Conferences and symposia	00005
	Education	00006
Management and Supervision	Line management	00007
	Project management	00008
Method and Systems Support	Year 2000	00009
	New clinical supplies planning system	00010
Support Services	Secretarial	00034
	Archiving	00042
	Facilities maintenance	00045
	Engineering maintenance	00046
Product Support	Product XXXX	00020
	Product YYYY	00016
	Product AAAA	00020
	Product BBBB	00025

Figure 6.2. A Weekly Timesheet

Date: 4 January 1999 **Week Number:** 1

Name: S. Jones **Personnel Number:** 160378

Department: Pharmaceutical Sciences—Inhalation Technology

Project	Project Code	Mon.	Tue.	Wed.	Thurs.	Fri.	Sat.	Sun.	Total
PN 12345	12345	8.0	4.0		4.0	3.0			19.0
PN 12034	12034								
PN 12367	12367								
PN 12563	12563								
PN 14575	14575								
PN 14523	14523								
PN 12366	12366								
PN 12452	12452		2.0	4.0	4.0	2.0			12.0
PN 13425	13425								
Annual holiday	00001								
Public holiday	00002								
Sickness	00003								
Training	00004	2.0							2.0
Management	00005								
	00016								
	00020								
	00025			2.0	1.0	2.0			5.0
	00010		3.0	2.0		1.0			6.0
Total		10.0	9.0	8.0	9.0	8.0			44.0

Management Reports

A number of management reports were produced from the system. Time spent on specific projects and comparisons of estimates and actual were considered to be the most useful for department managers (Figure 6.3). Department managers were also given a summary of the breakdown of work by category each month (Figure 6.4). A more detailed report of all activities and the number of hours spent on each activity (not illustrated) was also provided in support of the summary. With these reports, the managers could keep track of exactly what was happening in their departments.

When the system was first introduced, a number of surprises were experienced. It is often the laboratory supervisor who decides on the work being done on a day-to-day basis, not the department manager. In situations where resources were overloaded, it became apparent that the staff were responding to those project managers, regulatory officers and so on who shouted the loudest, not necessarily according to agreed-on priorities.

Function heads were provided with a breakdown of time used for each of the work categories defined earlier, and the R&D management committee also received a summary of time spent by category. This report, a simple histogram, showed the estimate for the year, the actual year to date and the actual for a given month (Figure 6.5).

The Fisons' system was not time-consuming to operate, although staff did complain that filling in a time sheet (or entering the information directly into a computer system) was a project activity in itself. These complaints disappeared when the system had been in use for awhile and because managers insisted on raising the issue with staff who regularly failed to complete their timesheet.

There were two major benefits from the system:

1. Managers were able to use the data to support additional resources (headcount or budget for contracting out certain activities) or to reduce the number of high-priority projects undertaken at a given time.

Figure 6.3. Time Usage Analysis: Project Estimate Versus Actual

Department: Pharmaceutical Sciences—Inhalation Technology June 1999

Project	Code	Hours This Month	Hours Last Month	Year to Date	Estimate 1999
Development					
Project 12345	12345				
Project 12367	12367				
Project 12396	12396				
Project 12329	12329				
Project 12034	12034				
Project 12563	12563				
Project 14575	14575				
Project 14523	14523				
Project 12366	12366				
Project 12452	12452				
Project 12460	12460				
Project 13425	13425				
Project 13426					
Research Projects					
Project 99934	99934				
Project 99946	99946				
Project 99947	99947				
Project 99950	99950				
Holiday and Sickness					
Public holiday					
Annual entitlement					
Sickness					

Figure 6.3 continued on the next page

Figure 6.3 continued from the previous page

Project	Code	Hours This Month	Hours Last Month	Year to Date	Estimate 1999
Training and Development					
Training					
Conferences and symposia					
Education					
Management					
Line management					
Project management					
Method Support					
Year 2000					
New clinical supplies planning system					
Support Services					
Secretarial					
Archiving					
Finance					
Engineering maintenance					
Product Support					
Product AAAA					
Product BBBB					
Product CCCC					
Product XXXX					
Product YYYY					

Figure 6.4. Time Usage Analysis by Department

Department: Pharmaceutical Sciences – Inhalation Technology
June 1999

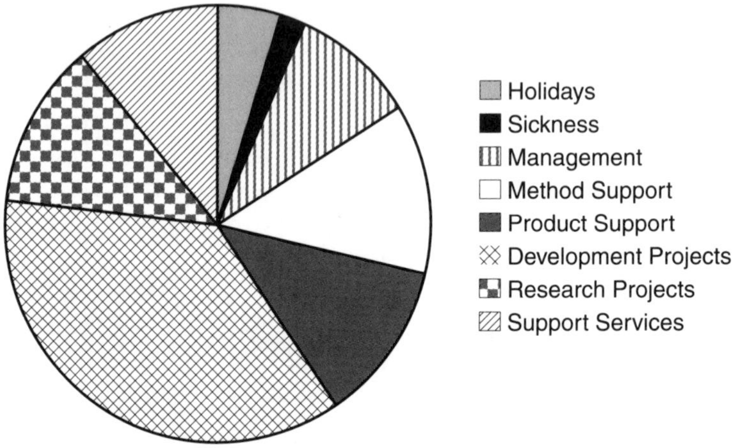

Figure 6.5. Time Usage Analysis: Work Category Analysis

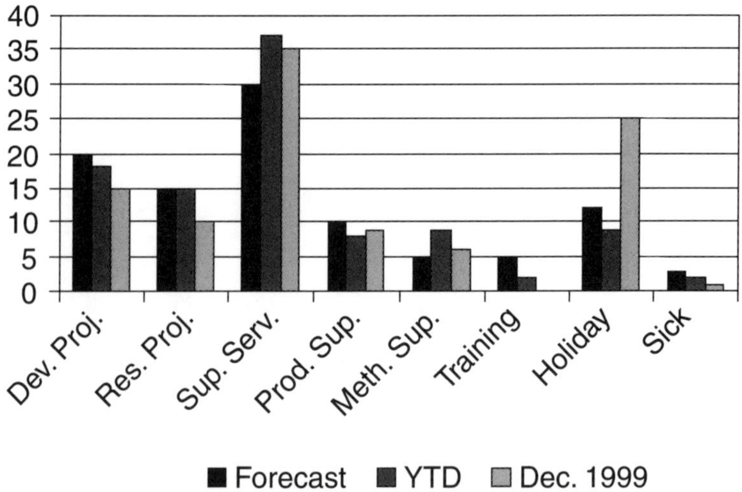

2. Experience in estimating the time for project activities improved project planning. It became apparent that managers were overly optimistic as to how much resources was actual needed for certain tasks. It became clear that repeating aspects of work, problem solving and troubleshooting were not adequately allowed for at the planning phase of the project.

7

Effective Programme Management Organisation

Earlier, programme management was defined as the process whereby projects are raised, assessed, approved, funded and implemented. To implement this concept effectively, an appropriate organisation must be in place.

There are three different functions (Figure 7.1) that need to be fulfilled in an effective organisation:

1. Development portfolio management
2. Project control
3. Project implementation

The organisation must fulfil these functions, and this can be achieved by forming two separate management teams whose scope will be described below; alternatively, a single management

Figure 7.1. Functions of Programme Management

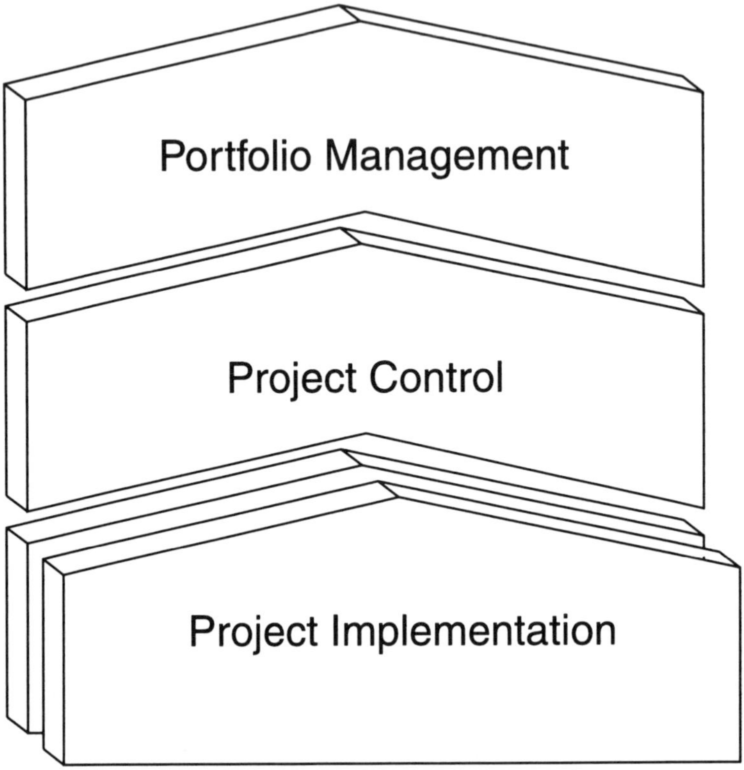

team can fulfil these functions. Whether one or two teams are constituted will depend on the size of the organisation, but the terms of reference must be clear, and roles and responsibilities must be well defined. Also, the key to effective management is access to good quality and timely information (Figure 7.2).

PORTFOLIO MANAGEMENT GROUP

The Portfolio Management Group is responsible for managing the development portfolio, which includes approval, termination

Figure 7.2. Programme Management Organisation

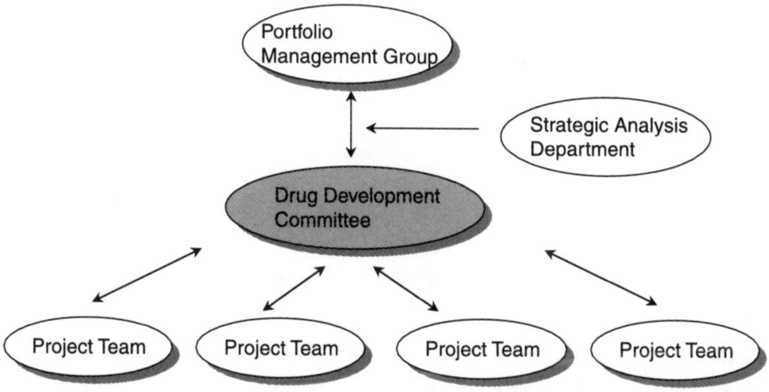

and prioritising of projects and the allocation of resources. This team should consist of the senior managers from drug development and corporate marketing. Clearly, job titles will vary according to the organisation but should include function heads responsible for the following functions:

- Clinical development
- Regulatory affairs
- Pharmaceutical sciences
- Preclinical safety
- Process chemistry
- Project management
- Corporate marketing
- Business development/licensing
- Industrialisation/technical operations (also responsible for technology transfer into manufacturing operations)

To be effective, these managers must function as a team committed to the consistent implementation of decisions particularly with respect to the delivery of resources and the application of agreed project priorities. Systems are required to provide the information for decision making (see Chapter 4).

DRUG DEVELOPMENT COMMITTEE

The role of the Drug Development Committee is essentially one of scientific management. It will provide guidance to project teams, approve project plans in terms of the development strategy and the studies to be undertaken and review projects at go/no go decision points with the project teams. Decisions will be taken as to whether projects should be progressed, re-planned or terminated at project decision points. Re-planning involves decisions which include a significant change in the scope of planned activities, such as the inclusion of an additional arm in the planned pivotal clinical studies or the addition of project activities which have a significant impact on the time-scale or cost of the project (e.g., changing the formulation to overcome side-effects or adding additional toxicology studies to investigate effects in additional species).

In a small organisation, the members of this team may be the same as the Portfolio Management Group; however, in larger organisations, this function can best be served, in some cases, by senior department managers rather than function heads. It also makes sense to divide the scientific management of projects according to therapeutic area since the appropriate individuals may be different (e.g., the clinical function member for a central nervous system project will not be the same as that for an anti-infective project). Similarly, the corporate marketing member may also be different.

Membership on the Drug Development Committee should include representatives from the following departments:

- Clinical Development
- Regulatory Affairs

- Clinical Pharmacology
- Pharmaceutical Sciences
- Biochemistry
- Drug Metabolism
- Statistics
- Preclinical Safety
- Process Chemistry
- Project Management
- Corporate Marketing
- Industrialisation/Technical Operations

The terms of reference include the following:

- Set project objectives.
- Appoint project team members.
- Approve project strategies and plans.
- Approve changes to strategies and plans as appropriate.
- Provide a challenge to the content of project plans to ensure consistency with the agreed project objectives.
- Approve target product profiles, minimum acceptable profiles and other acceptance criteria for critical project decision points.
- Ensure that appropriate technical standards are applied.
- Approve progression to the next phase of the project at major milestones.
- Terminate projects that do not meet acceptance criteria at major milestones.
- Make recommendations to the Portfolio Management Group if more resources are required.

This management team should not do the project team's job; they should not get involved in the technical detail other than to challenge the following:

- Content of plans (ensure that plans meet business objectives)
- Target product profile and minimum acceptable profile
- Other acceptance criteria

The focus should be on those technical issues that have been identified by the project team and on the challenge and approval of remedial plans to resolve the issues that will inevitably arise with all development programmes. If this group overturns the recommendations of the project team on a frequent basis, this is a symptom that the process is not working. In this case, communications should be improved, and the function heads should examine the calibre and experience of the project team members. If the team members are too inexperienced, inappropriate decisions can result. Also, the management of projects within line functions in terms of communications, for example, the appropriate involvement of department members and the quality of the science undertaken, should be reviewed, and corrective actions taken where necessary.

Project reviews held at major milestones and decision points along the project are essential to good project management. It is the role of this group to ensure that projects only progress to the next phase if the essential acceptance criteria are met. Otherwise it is appropriate to make one of the following recommendations to the programme management team:

- Repeat a significant element of the project.
- Do additional studies.
- Terminate the project.

Decisions to reformulate the product or to repeat a clinical programme at a different dose range may be appropriate; however, the impact of such decisions on time-scales, costs and ultimate sales revenues should be assessed in the same way as new projects are assessed.

PROJECT TERMINATION

The termination of projects in a timely fashion increases the productivity of development functions, minimising the expenditure on drug candidates that are not marketable (Figure 7.3). This objective check needs to be performed by the project teams because it can be difficult for individuals who have worked on a project with considerable commitment for many months or even years to accept that a project should be terminated. However, if the team has been involved in the determination of the acceptance criteria and the project leader keeps the focus of the team on the critical success criteria, an effective project team should recommend termination of projects as necessary.

Projects will be terminated if they do not meet the acceptance criteria as defined in the target profile or the minimum acceptable profile. These decisions are usually well accepted by project teams and members of senior management teams. However, it is important to review the commercial outlook for a potential product at each decision point, since it is quite possible that the environment has changed.

Figure 7.3. Project Termination

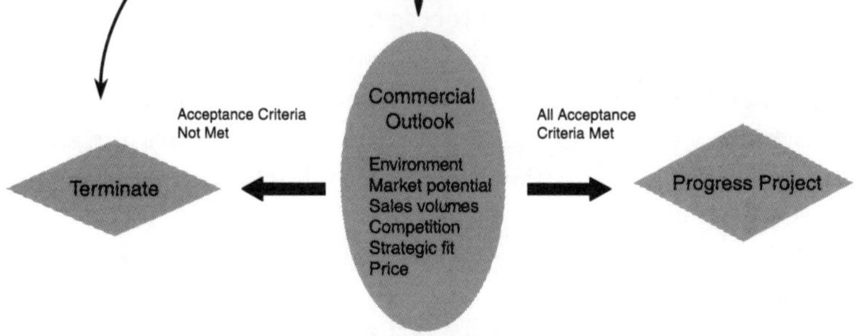

A competitor product may have been launched which has changed prescribing habits and the methods of treatment for a particular set of indications. Government legislation or regulatory guidelines may have been introduced which will ultimately affect sales. Forecasts may be revised downward to the point that the project is no longer attractive.

It is also possible that business strategies may have changed with respect to which therapeutic areas the organisation wants to continue, therefore, a potential product may simply no longer fit. In this case, the company may decide to sell the compound and to continue with an out-licence project rather than terminate it immediately, depending on the stage of development and how much data are available.

The reasons for termination may be difficult for some individuals to accept, and we are all aware of projects that will not lie down when they are dead. A number of years ago, I was involved in the decision to terminate a line extension project in development, and the business units did not agree with the decision. One local company affiliate found a way to continue product development using contract and local company technical resources. The product was launched in some European countries several years later. Unfortunately, it proved difficult to support from a manufacturing point of view because the process had not been optimised. Some critical aspects had not been fully understood, and the regulatory support was also very significant because the original dossier was weak.

This approach resulted in significant resources having to be deployed to support the product close to approval and after launch, and the projected sales were never met. The individuals who pursued this project firmly believed in its value, but the failure to adhere to a rigourous process to assess the value of projects resulted in a poor decision. R&D and business managers must remember that the decision to continue with a project has an opportunity cost. It may be better for a local company affiliate to allocate funds for additional promotional activities than to pursue projects of questionable value.

Conversely, I can also give an example of a more recent project where Corporate Marketing refused to support a particular development, which was funded by a local company affiliate.

This product was developed rapidly and was launched with no unexpected support being required. We have yet to see, however, whether in the longer term, the investment will prove to be justified.

Both of these examples illustrate that decisions can be right or wrong, and it is often not possible to gain commitment to the decision by everyone concerned. However, in my experience, the more information that is made available to support the decision to terminate a project, the greater the acceptance will be. An insistence on rigourous definition of target profiles and a good understanding of commercial and regulatory environments will not only help to reduce the number of bad decisions but also prove to be invaluable in gaining sufficient commitment to making the decisions stick.

PROJECT ANALYSIS DEPARTMENT

The formation of an analysis group is an essential staff function for programme management. This group ideally will consist of individuals who have the analytical skills and an understanding of the tools and techniques necessary to provide all the information required by the Portfolio Management Group.

The role of this department will be to undertake the following:

- Consolidate project plans.
- Complete project assessment at initiation and at go/no go decision points and present the results to the Portfolio Management Group.
- Manage the project resource management system and database.
- Manage the time recording system.
- Provide management information reports.
- Work with function heads and the Finance Department to prepare and present budgets.

These individuals will work with project teams to develop high-level project plans, resource estimates and financial and sales data for the initial project assessments.

This department will undertake the generation and analysis of the various scenarios mentioned earlier when strategic planning and portfolio management was discussed and information provided to the management committees for decision making. For the preparation of budgets, this department can provide department managers and function heads with headcount requirements based on the resource estimates for development projects and knowledge of the allocation of time to non-project activities.

PROJECT IMPLEMENTATION

A project team that is responsible for the development of project strategies and plans, including contingency planning, completion of all activities and progress monitoring and reporting undertakes project implementation. The following chapters will provide more information on the characteristics of highly effective project teams.

ROLE OF DEPARTMENT LINE MANAGER

In a matrix organisation, it is easy to see the role of management committees and project team members, but the role of the department manager in the project system can become blurred. Any confusion over roles is a potential cause of conflict; in particular, any confusion of management roles will be a cause of conflict between line managers and the project director. The line managers must be responsible for the following:

- Allocation of project team members
- Quality of scientific contribution to the project

- Allocation of resources to project
- Quality of documentation produced for regulatory submissions
- Budgeting

It is the responsibility of the project director to bring any shortcomings in the above areas to the attention of the department manager concerned, but it is not the project director's job to resolve the issues.

In pharmaceutical R&D, it is unusual for the project director to manage a project budget. Budgeting is the responsibility of the department manager. The project director is responsible for making sure that the project plan is sufficiently comprehensive so that the department manager has a good basis for the budget.

The role of the budget holder could be re-examined along with the role of the project leader (see Chapter 10). High calibre project leaders may be even more effective if they are free to make spending allocations. In particular, outsourcing certain project activities could be handled within the project team and result in more flexibility and faster problem solving.

Part Two

PROJECT MANAGEMENT

In my career, I have been involved in numerous projects in a number of different roles. These projects include drug development, technology transfer, new facilities design and build, quality improvements for marketed products, business re-engineering, the introduction of new technologies and even some systems development projects.

My role in these projects has ranged from specialist scientific team member, to project leader, to steering group member. Some projects were more successful than others. Even though the nature of the projects varied significantly, the characteristics of the most successful ones had a number of factors in common. The most significant of these factors are as follows:

- Clearly defined strategies
- Clearly defined objectives
- Clear and appropriate acceptance criteria
- Effective ways of working
- Inspirational project leader

- Effective project team
- Clear and well-defined project plans

Part two covers the management of individual projects and provides some ideas on how to improve the success of projects by addressing the factors summarised above. The use of project management software and the mechanisms of project planning will not be dealt with in detail since there are numerous excellent publications that deal with these mechanistic tools. Examples and anecdotes from actual projects are included to illustrate how development strategies, ways of working, project leadership and effective project teams can increase the business benefits delivered, reduce lead times and improve probability of success.

8

Development Strategy

The importance of setting very clear objectives and strategies should not be underestimated for drug development. I have heard it said that development cannot be planned any further than the next milestone, and objectives and strategies have to change according to the results of studies; therefore, there is no point investing too much resources on the development of comprehensive objectives, strategies and project plans.

In my experience, whatever the nature of the project (drug development programme, new facility design and build, a system development project, etc.), it is the amount of effort that is invested at the beginning of the project, to develop clear strategies and plans, which dictates the success of the outcome.

Fast track product development requires very clear project direction. It is true that strategies may change, and, of course, plans will have to be modified during the progression of a project. However, if a project does not have a clear direction from the start, there will be no basis for decision making and control over how the project progresses. Failure to develop a clear overall strategy for the project and for each of its critical elements often results in a final outcome which does not meet the expected business benefits. Here are some examples:

- A product fails to meet its sales forecasts due to ineffective positioning or differentiation.
- Because of manufacturing issues, there are problems with product supply following launch. These issues can arise from poorly designed processes or from an inappropriate manufacturing strategy.
- Unexpected adverse reactions occurred because the safety profile was not appropriately determined during development.
- Adverse events with special groups occurred because drug interactions or metabolism were not fully understood.

Most companies have had post-launch problems with new products. The most serious ones are patient safety issues and insufficient market penetration to recoup development and promotional costs. These products should either have been terminated during development, or a better definition of the product profile and unique selling points should have been established to enable appropriate product differentiation and positioning. Product differentiation is extremely important for pricing purposes, and the development programme must address this in terms of defining the mechanism of action, safety profile efficacy. Advantages over existing therapies must be clearly defined.

Recent examples of products that have been the subject of withdrawals are Tasmar® and Posicor®. Tasmar®, a product for the treatment of Parkinson's disease, was withdrawn from the market following issues with metabolism in certain patients, and Posicor® was withdrawn due to drug interactions.

What is important is that the number of expensive mistakes should be minimised in the future. Effective project management is the vehicle by which these mistakes can be minimised and hopefully avoided completely. Sir John Harvey Jones (a British industrialist and former chief executive of ICI) has been quoted as saying that "a majority of compounds which reach the market do not recoup their R&D [research and development] and early promotional costs."

Development strategies, therefore, must not only facilitate rapid drug development but also seek to eliminate non-competitive compounds as soon as possible. Clinical programmes should not only focus on obtaining regulatory approval but also address product differentiation and positioning. In this way, it is possible to maximise the business benefits from the R&D spend, to increase the effectiveness of resource utilisation and, ultimately, to maximise the profitability of those compounds that do reach the market-place.

Following the nomination of a compound for development, a project plan is prepared. The development strategy for the compound should provide the basis for the project plan, and, in my experience, insufficient consideration is often given to this strategy. In particular, the role of corporate marketing is often inadequate for reasons which will be explored later.

The consequences of not doing so include repetition of work, generation of poor quality reports, which lead to poor quality regulatory submissions, and the extended approval times which, if we are honest as managers in the industry, we have all experienced at some time.

This chapter gives some ideas on how to develop strategies that will help to eliminate many common problems, including

- the failure to terminate or late termination of non-competitive compounds,
- protracted development time-scales,
- insufficient product differentiation from competitor products,
- long regulatory approval times and
- poor product supply after launch.

DEVELOPMENT STRATEGIES

The selection of the development strategy for a compound depends on a number of factors.

Therapeutic Area

Clinical development strategies may have to differ according to therapeutic area. The definition of clinical endpoints, for example, will have an impact on the complexity of the clinical programme and will effect both the time to complete and the cost. Clinical endpoints are generally easier to define in the treatment of acute conditions than for the treatment of chronic conditions or degenerative diseases (e.g., those for anti-infective products are much easier to define than those for stroke or Alzheimer's disease).

The use of surrogate endpoints alone is becomingly increasingly difficult to justify to regulatory authorities. Chronic conditions and degenerative diseases may require mortality, quality of life or health economic studies in addition to surrogate measures. Such programmes can take considerable time to complete and require large patient numbers to ensure that enough patients remain in the study for follow-up.

Wherever efficacy can be demonstrated by short placebo-controlled or comparative studies, it may be possible to obtain regulatory approval on the basis of Phase 2 clinical studies. If Phase 3 studies are required, they can be completed with fewer patients on a shorter time-scale. Approaches such as these have been successful in the development of anti-infective products, in oncology and certain cardiovascular indications, including acute myocardial infarction.

Many companies are adopting development strategies that require only the clinical programme (and clearly the early preclinical studies) on the critical path to launch. This approach has the advantage of minimising time to market, but it has the following consequences:

- Carcinogenicity studies (for chronic indications) must be started early.

- The synthetic route for the drug substance must be frozen early.
- Technology transfer to manufacturing must also be started early, often with significant investment decisions having to be made for facilities and plants before efficacy is proven.

Competition

Speed of development will be influenced by competitor activity. Whether or not a compound is first or early in its class or whether it is a late entrant in an established class will influence the strategy on speed of development.

Where there is competition to be number two or three to market with a compound having a particular mechanism, potential market share can be greatly impacted. Being number three rather than number two will reduce market share significantly, unless the third entrant has very significant advantages over the previous two.

Identification of competitive advantages will be important for a compound in an established class, and rapid development will be essential if significant sales are to be secured. Fast track development will require parallel programmes, which increase costs and risk early on in development. A slower approach in which first studies in humans are completed before a commitment to long-term toxicology studies is made may be justified in more speculative areas where competition is not the biggest issue.

Number of Compounds in Development Portfolio

The amount of resources that can be devoted to any development candidate will depend on the number and relative business worth of other candidates in the portfolio (see Chapter 4).

STRATEGIC BUSINESS OBJECTIVES

Where appropriate, the design of the development programme should be consistent with strategic business objectives. Lead indications, dosage forms and product presentations should be compatible with strategic business plans, core business strengths, sales force capability and manufacturing strategy.

However, novel compounds may require modification to the existing business objectives of a company, if benefits from new research are to be realised or maximised. Flexibility and an iterative approach between the strategic business plan and the progress of the R&D portfolio should be maintained. The investment in New Chemical Entities (NCEs) can be fully exploited if follow-up developments such as line extensions and new product presentations are included in a long-term product life cycle management plan.

Probability of Success

More speculative developments, in diseases such as stroke, Parkinson's, Alzheimer's, dementia and so on may justify a more cautious approach in the early stages of development. Sequential rather than parallel programmes and allocating resources as milestones are reached until proof of concept is successfully completed are strategies that minimise risk and hence costs. However, if resources do allow a fast track development programme, the first compound to market with a new clinical benefit in these areas will secure significant market penetration and sales. The longer it takes for direct competitors to enter the market, the greater sales revenues will be. For compounds which are not first in a class, time to market is most critical in the determination of market share.

Market Forecasts

The fastest development strategies should be employed for those compounds that have the best combination of probability of success and projected sales. The selection of lead indications should include considerations of price, since the first price obtained will form a basis for pricing future presentations and line extensions. Indications which have the potential for obtaining orphan drug status should be developed as rapidly as possible, since regulatory approval times are likely to be shorter.

Resource Availability

Development resources should be allocated to projects according to potential business benefits (see Chapter 4).

Time to Market

Parallel programmes are more expensive but result in earlier launches for successful candidates. Each month saved on the time to launch represents one month's *peak sales*. For a blockbuster product, this could represent approximately $100 million.

At the time of nomination for development, there are two broadly different, alternative strategies for exploratory development:

1. Fast track to an early readout in humans, minimising the time and resources spent on development of a synthetic route and the production of quantities of drug substance, preclinical safety and formulation development.

2. Parallel programmes with early commitment to a significant preclinical safety programme and development of the synthetic route to provide quantities of drug substance sufficient to support it.

Option one will provide the fastest route to the first decision point. If successful, there will be a delay before Phase 2 can begin, since more preclinical work will be needed to support longer duration clinical studies. This approach will include doing sufficient preclinical work to support only Phase 1 studies. These studies may be of very short duration, requiring only 14-day studies in two species. Clearly, if the programme progresses beyond the first decision point, preclinical studies will be required, and a delay will be incurred before further clinical studies can be undertaken.

Option two will provide a fast track to Phase 2. For those compounds which do not progress beyond the first decision point in humans, more resources will have been expended than for option one.

Option two will almost certainly be faster to market, but a critical factor in early commitment to toxicology studies is the availability of the drug substance. For this reason, it is becoming increasingly common for resources to be allocated to developing a synthetic route before nominating a compound for exploratory development. If the synthesis of the drug substance is very difficult and/or expensive, option one may be appropriate, but some resources can still be allocated to the development of the drug synthesis should the outcome be positive for the compound.

Option one is appropriate to enable the best candidate for development to be chosen from a class or to select a single isomer for chiral compounds. It is also the best option for very novel compounds, targeting early studies which provide data in humans before significant resources are invested in chemical syntheses that are often difficult and expensive. The probability of success for novel compounds in a new class is likely to be lower than for compounds in an established class.

Option two may be the preferred option for compounds in an established class, since time to market must be minimised for optimal sales. This option is also more appropriate if the pharmacology predicts a significant therapeutic advantage over existing therapies or if the probability of success is higher than other opportunities.

The choice of strategy for exploratory development is dependent on a number of factors:

- Difficulty of chemical synthesis and availability of drug substance
- Novel compound—first in its class
- Chirality—choice of enantiomer for development
- Predictability of efficacy models and their relevance to humans

- The number of projects competing for the same resources
- Probability of success

The number of projects competing for the same resources is always a factor in the choice of fast track or alternative strategies, as we saw in the first part of this book. For regulatory development, clear strategies should be set for the following programmes

Clinical Development

Market research should be started early, and the following aspects of the clinical development strategy should be decided before the regulatory phase of development is undertaken.

- Selection of indications for first registrations, including consideration of acute versus chronic, adult and paediatric
- Target time-scale for Phases 2 and 3
- Dosage forms and package presentations
- Position on product life cycle management, which dictates the time-scale for line extensions (i.e., different strengths can be introduced at a later date, in line with long-term marketing plans)
- Definition of types of clinical endpoints required

The Phase 2 clinical programme is the cornerstone of the drug development programme and is most critical to the long-term success of a drug in the market-place. Dose selection and dosage regimen determination are critical, as are knowledge of pharmacokinetics and the effect of the drug in special groups (i.e., renal or hepatic compromised patients, etc.).

It is often tempting to reduce the time and effort on Phase 2, seeking only to demonstrate efficacy. Definitive dose ranging, dose regimen and, in some cases, comparative studies are important in that they provide the best platform for Phase 3. Many drugs currently on the market have not reached their maximum sales potential due to inadequate dose definition during Phase 2.

Inclusion of comparative studies in Phase 2 will, in some cases, lead to the termination of projects for compounds that will not be competitive in the market-place. In today's costly and competitive environment, it makes good sense to spend more in Phase 2, such that only candidates with the highest probability of success are progressed to Phase 3.

Probability of success means compliance with safety, efficacy and sales targets. In the past, safety and efficacy targets have been the sole criteria for Phases 2 and 3, which has resulted in many compounds reaching the market that have not justified their development and promotional costs.

Preclinical Development

The preclinical development strategy will depend on the clinical strategy and the desired time to market. Early administration in man for up to 10 days will require 1-month toxicology studies; three- and six-month studies can be combined to support a longer duration of treatment. Chronic administration will require long-term studies, including carcinogenicity. These studies can be taken off the critical path to New Drug Application (NDA) submission by starting them early. In some cases, the carcinogenicity studies may need to start before the proof of concept studies are complete.

The availability of the drug substance can have an impact on the timing for certain studies. Specific observations during the clinical programme may require additional studies to be performed, such as drug interaction, safety pharmacology and so on.

Japanese requirements for toxicology studies can be integrated or run as separate programmes; these programmes are often conducted in Japan. This approach has significant implications for cost and time-scales for the start of clinical programmes in Japan. Integration of Japanese requirements into a core toxicology programme requires early collaboration with the Japanese affiliate or partner.

PRODUCT DESIGN

The final formulation must be developed for pivotal toxicity studies and clinical studies. Simple rapid-to-develop formulations are usually selected for exploratory development, but the parallel development of the final formulation is necessary for fast track development programmes.

A single formulation and single pack, ideally with one internationally accepted brand name, is the most desirable for a single indication (excluding adult and paediatric doses and sample packs) from a cost of goods perspective. This consideration has to be balanced against the needs of the various key markets; in particular, a single international brand name is difficult to achieve.

At the design stage, a trade-off is often made, in terms of time to market and cost of goods, between simple formulations and technologies and more complex alternatives. Simple formulations may offer little in terms of competitive advantage or as a barrier to entry for generic competition but will maximise speed to market. More sophisticated technologies and delivery systems may offer competitive advantage, but their development will be are more resource intensive, will require higher levels of expertise and increase the cost of goods.

Product life cycle management is important. Marketing and product development working together can generate a number of scenarios that can be implemented at different times.

For example, consider a sterile solution for injection. One option for product design is a terminally sterilised ampoule. This option is low risk and relatively straightforward to develop and industrialise. A second option may be a pre-filled syringe. This option is more complicated since sterilisation is more complex; a device will increase the cost of goods, and specialised filling and packaging equipment will be required in manufacturing. The selection of the syringe will be important, and special features may be needed for stability purposes.

The second option may be an advantage only in some markets. The pre-filled syringe could be developed for the first launch, or it could be a line extension which is introduced in some markets at a later date. Similarly, products which are intended for long-term therapy, such as hormone replacement therapy and contraception, lend themselves to novel delivery systems such as patches, gels and implants. These presentations can confer advantages in certain market segments over a tablet formulation, and life-cycle management is important to maximise market share and profitability.

There are many differences between U.S., Japanese and European markets that should be considered at the product design stage. There are formulation preferences, for example, tablets versus capsules and capsule sizes. In the United States, it is common for drugs to be formulated in size 0 capsules; in Europe, this size is considered to be too large, and patients object to taking them.

In Japan, ophthalmic products are sold in clear bottles so that they can be visually inspected for particles; in the United States and Europe, there is a market preference for opaque bottles for multidose presentations. In Europe and to some extent in the United States, there is a growing awareness of the environment, and environmentally friendly packaging and devices are becoming increasingly required.

The use of preservatives for certain presentations, and for ophthalmic products in particular, is becoming less popular in Northern Europe. For this reason, single-use preparations are being developed as well as multidose preservative-free presentations. These developments will increase manufacturing costs, and clear demonstration of superior safety will be required if higher prices are to be obtained to offset the cost of goods increase.

Clearly, it is in the interest of the business to minimise the number of variants in a product range. Production costs will be lower, and maintenance costs will also be lower (fewer package changes to control, fewer stability programmes, less components and suppliers to monitor, etc.). Local marketing departments will want to design a product for optimal sales in their market and will usually prefer different presentations in some. This is important for a corporate marketing strategy, which takes into account local needs but also keeps the product range under control.

Cost of goods is becoming more of an issue as governments move to contain drug costs by imposition of tougher pricing policies. Preferred manufacturing technologies will dictate aspects of product design. If policies on technologies exist within the company, these must be considered at the design stage.

There are no right or wrong approaches to the design of a product range; it depends on the business strategy of the company and the therapeutic area. There will be different benefits and costs associated with a range of options. What is in the interest of the business is to evaluate the cost/benefit of the various options and for decisions to be made after understanding the issues. Good quality data are required on the possible options, and good quality market research completed early is essential.

A mistake that many companies make is not to consult with the major markets early enough in the development process, which in particular can lead to last minute changes being made to both primary and secondary packaging late in the development programme. While secondary packaging changes can be made without impact on launch time-scales, late changes to primary packaging require stability studies and can lead to a short shelf life at launch.

PROCESS DEVELOPMENT

Primary

The primary process development is on the critical path to pivotal toxicology studies. As more complex molecules are being developed, syntheses are becoming more difficult, and yields are often low. It is becoming more and more common for the primary process development to begin pre-nomination in order to achieve the most rapid development times. Involvement of process chemists at the discovery stage can save many months of development time.

Technology transfer to a manufacturing plant at an early stage to facilitate manufacture for pivotal clinical trials is becoming more common. In particular, if the final stages which can impact the physical properties of the drug substance are produced at the manufacturing site, the need for bioequivalence studies prior to launch can be avoided.

Contract manufacture is being increasingly used to avoid large capital outlays before the safety and efficacy of a compound are known. Working with contractors is very demanding in terms of project management and requires good documentation of development work and excellent teamwork on behalf of the process chemists.

One way in which companies are maintaining manufacture in-house whilst minimising capital investment is a move to modular chemical plants. Modules are designed and commissioned for key syntheses, and additional capacity is obtained by adding another identical module. In this way, up to two years can be saved in the scale-up and transfer to operations of drug substances.

Secondary

The choice of technology will impact the speed of industrialisation and cost of goods. If Phase 3 clinical supplies are to be provided from the site of manufacture, standardisation of technologies in certain areas, e.g., tablet manufacture, sterilisation methods, aerosol manufacture and so on, will improve flexibility and reduce commercialisation costs.

Product design must be frozen before pivotal clinical studies and the NDA stability programme. Again, early technology transfer to the launch site for the manufacture of phase 3 clinical supplies will avoid the requirement for bioequivalence studies and provide more assurance of manufacturing capability at the time of a PAI (pre-approval inspection)

Process development must address the issue of design for manufacture and health and safety requirements, e.g., COSHH (Control of Substances Hazardous to Health) and SHE (safety, health and environmental) assessments should be done at an early stage in development. Current timings for PAIs and reductions in U.S. approval times necessitate that process development and analytical transfers be done much earlier than in the past. The early analytical methods transfers require involvement of the site Quality Control Laboratory at least 12 to 14 months prior to regulatory filings.

MARKETING

The launch platforms for the United States, Europe and Japan need to be developed early. The target profile and minimum acceptable profiles are required by the start of Phase 2, and an understanding of the market requirements for the United States, Europe and Japan, both current and future, is essential for this purpose. Positioning against the competition is an important input to the design of Phase 2 and 3 clinical programmes in order to ensure that an appropriate definition of competitive advantage, health economic criteria and so on are included.

The design of Phase 3B and Phase 4 clinical studies are critical to the success of new product launches. If the product is the first entrant in a new class, publications are required to help physicians identify suitable patients and to answer questions concerning safety and advantages over existing therapies. For later entrants in an existing class, comparative studies will be required to demonstrate clinical advantages, which are not necessarily required for licence approvals.

Branding and brand image has not traditionally been considered important by pharmaceutical companies for prescription medicines, although its importance is recognised for over-the-counter (OTC) medicines. The development of a strong brand is now becoming more important, particularly since the advent of substitution at the pharmacy. A brand image should be developed from the beginning, and early registration of brand names is important. Product life cycle management should be considered early, and a long-term programme for the introduction of line extensions after first launches should be developed.

The marketing strategy should be developed as the result of forward thinking. Too often, the market analysis is retrospective and does not predict the future. Political trends, economic activity and regulations are all factors that have an impact on product acceptance.

Current economic trends are indicating that South America will grow in importance over the next decade. What plans does your company have to take advantage of this?

REGULATORY

The regulatory strategy must include the route for approval in Europe, i.e., mutual recognition or central applications. The strategy should address whether a single core dossier that meet the needs of the United States, Europe and Japan will be targeted, or whether the Japanese programmes will be run separately. Local requirements for clinical studies and expert reports need to be clearly addressed as appropriate.

In some therapeutic areas and in some countries, it may be possible to obtain approvals for limited indications on the basis of Phase 2 clinical studies (certain anti-infective and oncology products). These possibilities need to be identified early, and a dialogue started with the regulatory authorities concerned.

There is one other important point to focus on: launch dates are what really matters, not filing dates. Over the years, I have seen NDA and marketing authorisation application (MAA) submissions made with dossiers that are deficient in one area or another, resulting in long approval times.

Have you ever heard the expression, "We can start the clock ticking and have our answers ready for the questions?" If this is an approach you are currently taking, make sure that you are being realistic about the questions, that the resources to generate the additional data are in place and that the answers will be available at the right time. The regulatory department must be the gatekeeper of the submission strategy and the quality of the dossier.

Poor forecasting for approval dates is very expensive. An unrealistic launch date results in inaccurate budget forecasts for sales, profits and promotional activities for the product concerned; it can also lead to decisions being taken which impact on the sales of products that are currently available.

I attended three launch conferences over two years for one product in one market because the regulatory approval time was completely underestimated. This resulted in unnecessary expenditures, and promotional resources were taken from other products that could have increased sales revenue. Realistic estimates of approval dates are required for good business decision making.

When the dossier is being compiled, the submission strategy must be thought through carefully in light of the data. There is no such thing as a perfect dossier, and we should not be too concerned about questions arising. However, when questions are received, the data to support the answers must be available. If there are significant deficiencies in the dossier at the planned submission date, approval may be obtained earlier by submitting a little later, with a higher quality dossier.

MANUFACTURING STRATEGY

Primary

For the first source, the choice between in-house or contract manufacture will depend on the process and the fit with current manufacturing capability, capacity available and the implications for investment. If considerable investment is required in plant before Phase 2 studies have been completed, outsourcing may be appropriate. Sourcing policy is becoming increasingly important in maintaining the low cost of goods. Make or buy decisions, whether to invest in modular plants and where to locate manufacturing facilities, are all important aspects of manufacturing and sourcing strategies. Outsourcing is a low-cost initial option, but control of critical manufacture is in the hands of someone else, and industrial property is being shared with potential suppliers for future generic competitors. Here partner management is crucial, and contracts need to be developed which protect industrial property as much as is possible.

The development of a supply strategy for five years after launch based on contract manufacture and building strategic stocks is one way to minimise investment in new plants before efficacy and the long-term sales potential are both fully understood. For companies with substantial in-house primary manufacturing capacity, investment in modular plants is one way to increase flexibility and minimise early investment in the new plant.

Good Manufacturing Practice (GMP) issues are more difficult to control, and the increasing attention given by the U.S. Food and Drug Administration (FDA) to drug substance manufacture makes outsourcing more of a risk and requires considerable input from Process Development, Quality Assurance and the Supply Chain to ensure good contractor selection. In some cases with specialist chemistry there may be only one or two suitable companies who can manufacture the required quantities.

Secondary

The selection of the launch manufacturing site is important, since changes can take up to three years to secure approvals after launch. Make or buy decisions should be made early. If in-house facilities are chosen, location is important to profitability. Tax advantages can be gained from manufacturing in certain countries.

Ideally, Phase 3 clinical supplies should be manufactured at the site of manufacture, on essentially similar manufacturing equipment, to ensure that no issues arise with process differences for launch. Most companies now require that the launch site be FDA approved and capable of producing at least three years' projected volume. A second source is usually required for large-volume products within a three-year time-frame.

In the past, many countries have required local manufacture to secure reimbursement and pricing. Overcapacity in the industry is a huge overhead burden, and many companies are looking at alternatives to local manufacture in Italy, Spain and some South American countries. These alternatives include R&D or local packaging only.

Inclusion of a second source for the manufacture of pivotal clinical trials will allow dual sourcing from launch (in the United States), however, the costs involved in two transfers before clinical efficacy is proven is prohibitive, and, therefore, most companies have a single source for three years or so after first launch. If considered appropriate, strategic stocks can be held to offset supply risks during this time.

9

Smart Development Methods

The pharmaceutical industry is consolidating at an increasing pace. The latest mergers between Astra and Zeneca and Hoechst Marion Rousell and Rhône Poulenc Rorer (Aventis) are but more examples of the rapid changes being brought about by the need to increase shareholder value. One of the drivers for such mergers is to increase the ability of research and development (R&D) to bring innovative products to market, since this is what is required to grow profits as patents expire, development costs escalate and competition intensifies.

The ability to put huge resources into R&D is not, however, the only critical success factor, and this is particularly so in drug development. To be successful in development in today's competitive environment requires companies to be smart. In my experience, development ways of working, project leadership and teamwork are more important than resource availability alone. Project leadership and effective project team working will be discussed in Chapters 10 and 11, respectively. Here ideas are presented to improve the effectiveness of development programmes by examining the ways of working.

The objective of pharmaceutical development is to bring a flow of products to the market in a manner which maximises sales and profits. Development programmes should be managed in a systematic way, with a major emphasis on scientific excellence, clear objective setting and the use of sound methodology that supports good experimental design, clear decision making and rapid problem solving.

There are a number of critical success factors that must be fulfilled in order to maximise sales and profits:

- Rapid development
- Rapid regulatory approvals
- Clear product differentiation and positioning
- Competitive pricing
- Publications which support product positioning at time of launch

Development projects should be managed in such a way that these critical success factors are met consistently.

Rapid development needs clear strategies (discussed in Chapter 9) and plans and the development of smart ways of working. Rapid regulatory approvals will not be possible if the quality of the dossier is not high and if corners have been cut for the sake of speed. Rapid development cannot exclude sufficient work to define the unique selling points to allow competitive product positioning and pricing. Clinical studies pivotal to the positioning and differentiation of the product must be published before launch.

So how can projects be managed such that all of these requirements are met? The project team should be directed to ensure that the following are in place for the project:

- Clear objectives and plans for each stage of the project
- Acceptance criteria set for milestones that define competitive advantage
- Appropriate cross-functional input to acceptance criteria

- Sound experimental design to provide good information for decision making
- Rigourous approach to problem solving
- Project team performance monitoring

Setting clear objectives for the project and for each stage within the project forms a basis for the development of a project plan. Exploratory development and full commercial development must have well-defined objectives and plans. When a strategy has been agreed for part of the development programme, specific objectives can then be set for each element of project. *The primary project objective should include a statement of the product dosage form and route of administration, indications, key markets, quality standards, cost of goods and time-scale.*

It is not always possible to specify indications definitively at the start of exploratory development, since models of efficacy or confirmation of the mechanism of action may still be under exploration. However, a broad definition of indications of business interest will be extremely useful in setting acceptance criteria as the project progresses.

ACCEPTANCE CRITERIA

All major milestones and decision points should be clearly defined, with acceptance criteria decided, before the studies leading to those milestones are designed. These acceptance criteria should form the basis for all studies that follow. The studies themselves must be well designed, and success criteria must be clearly defined for each study that are consistent with the acceptance criteria defined for the milestone decision point.

It is this definition of acceptance criteria at the start of each stage of the project that is an essential input to study design and to the generation of meaningful data upon which good decisions can be made. I have lost count of the number of times that a project review has been held at a major milestone where data have been presented which raise as many questions as they answer.

How many regulatory affairs managers complain that clinical reports, pharmaceutical development reports and so on are poor or just not adequate for regulatory submission?

How can the project team set clear acceptance criteria? There is nothing complex nor difficult about setting these criteria, but it does depend on taking a systematic approach to the identification of all milestones that need them. Equally important is the involvement of all the relevant team members such that a broad approach is taken, including marketing and manufacturing issues, and that the emphasis is not only on preclinical safety, clinical safety and efficacy. Properly defined acceptance criteria will include all areas where competitive advantages are required to ensure that the compounds which are brought to market are commercially successful.

A target profile for a drug candidate is usually set at the beginning of exploratory development and revised before the regulatory development phase. It is used mainly to influence both product design and the clinical programme. In addition, a minimum acceptable profile is often set and forms the basis of decision making at major milestones. The target and minimum acceptable profiles are sets of acceptance criteria but often only cover those clinical and safety aspects that define go/no go decision points. Typically, the target profile for an indication will consist of the following criteria:

- Patient population
- Route of administration
- Dosing regimen
- Efficacy targets
- Safety targets
- Cost of goods
- Quality targets

The inclusion of cost of goods targets and specific quality targets will not influence project go/no go decisions necessarily but will be helpful in aiding product and process design and eliminating options during the development process. Smart development requires acceptance criteria to be set for all aspects of development and some examples are given below.

Product Design

Acceptance criteria should be set for in the following areas as appropriate: formulation performance, including aspects effecting product safety and tolerability; bioavailability; number of doses; shelf life; patient compliance; quality; manufacturability; and cost of goods.

Design for manufacture is an aspect that can save time and cost when the product is being transferred into manufacturing. Acceptance criteria should be set with manufacturing in mind for products that include delivery systems or complex packaging requirements.

Process Design

Setting acceptance criteria for process capability, robustness, safety and cost of goods will allow options to be selected which maximise the efficiency of the process and, therefore, the profitability of the product at launch. This does not mean that the manufacturing process should be completely optimised before the first launch batches are made and that further improvements will not be necessary, but it will ensure that Good Manufacturing Practice (GMP) standards and batch reject or process wastage rates are acceptable at the time of first launches. Current regulatory environments do not allow for fragile processes that are difficult to control in routine manufacture.

Process capability can be measured statistically (CpK). If critical process parameters can be controlled to a CpK of 1.33 or greater, process validation will be successful, and failure rates in manufacturing will extremely low. A process capability of less than 1.0 will result in validation and/or stability failures.

Preclinical Safety and Toxicology

Safety and toxicology targets are almost always set appropriately, since regulatory reviewing mechanisms have provided sound guidelines on toxicity over many years. Few project teams have difficulty in taking decisions and making go/no go recommendations on the basis of toxicity.

Clinical Programmes

Target profiles form a starting point for experimental design for Phase 2 and 3 studies. The target profile is essentially a set of acceptance criteria or a set of questions that need to be answered. For example, if the target profile requires once-daily dosing, then the questions to be answered are, "Does the drug work at one or two doses per day?" "At what dose does the drug work once a day?"

Clinical development plans can be written to define in broad terms the number and design of each study to be undertaken, including the number of patients to be entered and the number of centres. Patient numbers are calculated according to the nature of the clinical endpoint and the minimum size of the difference required to be identified between placebo or comparator drug, for example.

The design of the clinical study protocols, diary cards and case report forms are critical to the quality of the data collected during the study. Most particularly, the speed with which centres are closed down and the time taken for statistical analysis and subsequent reporting of the study is dependent on good study design.

How often have clinical research associates (CRAs) been chasing queries and trying to fill in gaps in data many weeks after the last patient "completed"? Not only do these delays in closing down centres add to clinical development times, but there must be questions on the reliability of data collected several weeks after the treatment day in question. Detailed identification of the data to be collected during the clinical study and agreement on the format for data entry and methods analysis with the statistician before the design and format of case report forms and diary cards are finalised, has a number of benefits.

Record forms should be designed to be completed in the order in which data are collected. Only data which are required for analysis will be collected. (How many tomes are written unnecessarily taking many man-hours to unravel?) Rapid data entry upon completion of the first few patients aids valuable feedback by the statistician to the CRA, who can then resolve any issues, such as misunderstanding of the instructions.

I have seen examples of huge case report forms which were poorly structured—the information to be entered into the database by the biostatistician was scattered throughout the form instead of being collected logically. One particular report form asked for information in the form of comments, which the statistician did not understand. To summarise a long story, one centre took 21 weeks to close down following completion of the last patient. The design of the form made it difficult for the CRA to see omissions, and many queries had to be resolved weeks afterward, much to the frustration of the investigator, CRA and statistician.

Direct data entry in the clinic is possible with well-designed systems and is becoming popular as one method of reducing lead times for the completion of clinical studies. Electronic case report forms (CRFs) are being used by many pharmaceutical companies and contract research organizations (CROs). There are many software products available to support clinical trial design and reporting. British Telecom has a clinical trials system, and the company will also provide Internet services.

PROCESS DESIGN AND SCALE–UP

A process should be designed for the cost-effective manufacture of a good quality product. Quality and cost considerations dictate that the process should be robust and have minimal waste and acceptable lead times. The important steps include

- selection of appropriate technology;
- specifications and acceptance criteria for design, selection and approval of equipment;

- identification of critical process parameters; and
- process capability.

Effective ways of working for the project team should include challenges in each of these key areas.

Selection of Technology

The following questions should be answered before selecting a technology?

- Is it appropriate?
- Is the equipment supplier reputable and reliable?
- How tried and tested is it?
- What alternatives have been considered?
- Is the technology new to the company?

Ideally, the technology selected should not be new to the company, since dealing within unfamiliar technology will inevitably take longer while both development and manufacturing personnel progress through the learning curve.

Definition of Equipment Specifications

The first step is to define the user requirements, including volume, capacity, performance levels, cost of goods, level of automation, quality levels, wastage rates, environmental factors, safety and handling, training and operating skill requirements, maintenance and operating costs.

A functional specification derived from the user requirements can then be used to form the basis of the engineering specification. Equipment purchased for secondary manufacture falls into one of the following categories:

- Off the shelf
- Off the shelf and modified
- Custom built

Sufficient attention to the functional and engineering specifications must be given for modifications to off-the-shelf and for custom-built equipment. The performance specifications will form the basis of installation and operational qualifications.

Definition of Critical Process Parameters and Process Capability

Good experimental design and the generation of sufficient data to calculate process capability (Cp and CpK) will form a good basis for the development of robust processes. The following areas should be challenged:

- Have all critical parameters been identified?
- Is the size of the database sufficient?
- Have in-process controls been identified?
- Have maintenance procedures been identified?

WAYS OF WORKING

Over many years of working in R&D and technical operations, I have spent a lot of time observing and improving ways of working to make project implementation more effective. Below are some examples of approaches to ways of working which improve both the efficiency and effectiveness of project implementation.

Experimental Design

For every day spent in thinking about experimental designs, the statistical method of analysis and the definition of endpoints, weeks and even months can be saved at the end of the project. The quality of the information generated for decision making is increased exponentially, and the quality of reports for regulatory submissions is also improved.

What does this mean in practical terms? Setting clear objectives for the programme based on the acceptance criteria in the target profile is the starting point for the experimental design.

I have seen numerous examples where data have been generated because it seemed like a good idea but added no value to the experiment. Only data required to answer the questions dictated by the acceptance criteria should be collected. Additional data may not lead to a conclusion but since all data have to be reported, complexity is added that is not necessarily helpful.

Poor statistical design may result in the generation of data that cannot be interpreted. A common mistake is to measure the right parameters, but insufficient data points are available to draw a solid conclusion. Sample size and power of studies need to be carefully considered when experiments and studies are designed.

For example, I encountered one experiment which compared the properties of two materials for a component of a product pack. Due to the availability of materials at the beginning of the experiment, different sample sizes were chosen for the components. In one test, a single out-of-specification result was obtained in the larger sample, and none were observed in the other sample group.

Were these materials equivalent? Clearly, it is not possible to answer that question from the data set. The experiment was repeated with equal sample sizes, but because of the natures of the test and the process lead times involved, the repetition added several weeks to the project time-scale.

I have seen cases where clinical studies have been conducted with insufficient power to differentiate the active from the placebo (in the allergy area, placebo effects can be high, and study designs should allow for this) or between the drug candidate and the active comparator. Giving due consideration to the patient numbers required is essential particularly in therapeutic areas where the placebo effect is high or where the evaluation of competitive advantage for a specific parameter is important to the outcome of the study.

The target profile is an important consideration for the design of Phase 2 studies. One example, which illustrates this issue well, was the design of a Phase 2 study for an allergy product. The target profile contained a requirement for once-daily dosing, and a study was designed that compared an active given once per day to a placebo. There was considerable discussion by the project team as to whether this simple design was most appropriate. Alternatives, which included a twice-daily arm or an active comparator, were discussed and recommended, but the project steering committee (R&D function heads) took the decision to keep the design simple for speed to market.

The study was completed, and efficacy was demonstrated at once-a-day dosing as compared with placebo. However, the physician leading the clinical programme was not convinced that the primary variable showed sufficient improvement over the placebo in order to be competitive in the market-place. A decision was taken to repeat the study, and this time an active comparator was included in the study design. The second study showed efficacy over placebo but did not satisfy comparative efficacy requirements at the preferred dose regimen; comparative efficacy could only be achieved with twice-daily dosing.

As a result of this study, the project was terminated on the grounds that profitability targets for the product were unlikely to be met. This decision could have been made a year earlier if the original study design had been different. The costs of continuing the entire programme for a year longer than necessary were much greater than the costs of adding another arm to the original Phase 2 study.

This example illustrates some important points:

- The design of Phase 2 studies must take into account all relevant aspects of the target profile if the best decisions are to be made. The target profile must be clearly written such that all requirements are clearly stated and understood. Similarly, the minimum acceptable profile must be clearly defined at the time of go/no go decisions.

- The project team understood the issues but failed to convince the management team. This was done in a culture which did not empower the teams; managers who had less understanding of all the issues and risks did too much decision taking.

- A development strategy which sets rigourous acceptance criteria at Phase 2 is one that will help reduce overall development costs, by eliminating compounds or line extensions which do not have sufficient competitive advantage. The short-term results will, however, be increased costs at Phase 2.

The design of Phase 2 clinical studies is an area that deserves particular attention: Determination of the appropriate dose and dosage regimen can have a significant impact on the success of the product. For many products already on the market, the dose and/or the regimen have not been optimised with respect to efficacy and safety. In the haste to achieve minimum development times, many companies do less work in Phase 2 than is necessary if these parameters are to be optimised.

It may well be cost-effective to get to market quickly with a suboptimal dose or dosage regimen and to follow up with additional studies after launch to justify changes in labelling. However, there is a risk that choosing the wrong dose for the Phase 3 programme will compromise efficacy or clinical safety, resulting in delays in obtaining regulatory approval while additional studies are performed. In extreme cases, the Phase 3 programme may need to be repeated with a different dose. Using a structured approach to experimental design, scientific methods such as hypothesis testing and statistical methods will improve the quality of development work significantly and reduce time-scales.

This book will not go into a lot of detail here, but a project team that is effectively lead and prompted to use these structured approaches will find many ways of improving ways of working in all areas of development. Some examples are given below.

Planning and Thinking Time

Insufficient time is often given to planning precisely what needs to be done. On one occasion, I asked a team member for the plan for a particular project activity and was told that he did not have time to plan—he just had to get on with it.

Spend a moment or two thinking about the implications of that statement. If he did not have the time to plan what he was going to do and how it was to be done, how could I have any confidence in his results? There are two explanations for this type of approach, either he was under so much time pressure that he was making up the plan as he went along, or there was insufficient discipline in the department such that good, solid, scientific methodology was not required.

Unfortunately, this is not a unique example. Although we consider ourselves proficient scientists, we often do not put enough effort into thinking through what needs to be done. All too often, the result is not enough time is allowed to get it right, but, ironically, there is always time to do it again when the first plan did not work out.

As senior managers, we should examine our own role in this type of issue. There is no question that projects must be implemented as rapidly as possible in today's competitive environment, but getting it right the first time is always cheaper and faster than doing it twice. Too much pressure for speed sometimes has the opposite result. Those managers who insist on excellence will be the most successful in the long run. Sir John Harvey Jones once said:

> Planning is an unnatural process! It is much more fun to do something. The nicest thing about not planning is that failure comes as a complete surprise, rather than being preceded by periods of worry and depression.

Good Product Design

For products that include delivery systems such as multidose pumps, pre-filled syringes, inhalation or other devices, consideration to ergonomics and value engineering confer significant benefits on the project. Ergonomic studies can be helpful in optimising the design of devices from a patient perspective.

Other tools such as failure modes and effects analysis (FMEA) can be used to challenge a device design and predict modes of malfunction, allowing quality assurance to be built in at the design stage. If FMEA is used on a model of a device, or on components from a single cavity development tool, before tooling is commissioned, a lot of time and expense can be saved by reducing the need for modifications later in the project. In some cases, tooling without sufficient challenge to the design can lock in poor features and quality problems for the lifetime of the product.

Ergonomics is a much-neglected area in the design of delivery systems, devices and packaging, but it has the potential to confer considerable competitive advantage, thus making the resulting design more attractive to patients. There are a number of companies and university departments that will undertake ergonomic studies on a contract basis, so it is not necessary to develop the expertise within the company.

Value engineering is of enormous value in the selection of design options that will impact on the functionality and usability of the device and development time-scales. Value engineering is a tool that will help designers select essential features and distinguish the "nice to haves". The cost of goods implications can be identified for all features, and the information enables a design to be derived which optimises functionality for a minimum cost. The time-scales for development are usually impacted by the complexity of the device or component; features that are not considered to be essential but nice to have can add significant time to the development programme.

At some point, it may be more cost-effective to get version one of a device to market more quickly without some of the nice to haves and improve the product by adding additional features after launch in version two. Additional features can be built into subsequent versions while the first version is on the market earning revenue and gaining market share. Subsequent introductions of the improved versions can serve to increase sales and extend product life cycles.

Again, there are many consultancy companies which specialise in these techniques. It is not necessary or desirable to develop the skills in-house—an independent assessment is extremely beneficial. It is necessary, however, to have an appreciation of the techniques and the benefits which can be conferred by their timely and appropriate use and to have the skills in-house to manage consultants.

10

Project Leadership

The first prerequisite for an effective project team is the appointment of a high calibre project leader. The calibre of the team members is also very important, as is the size and structure of the core project team. The critical roles of the project leader will be explored in this chapter. Chapter 11 will discuss project team effectiveness and structure.

THE EFFECTIVE PROJECT LEADER

Excellence in the leadership of projects is an essential element in project management, and it is an area that does not always get the attention it deserves. Sir John Harvey Jones has been quoted as saying that "leadership is the ability to achieve the extraordinary with ordinary people". The pharmaceutical industry employs many extraordinarily talented people but often underachieves in drug development. Could this be due to a lack of leadership?

Personally, I think it is. A single leader is often never appointed; instead, a focus is placed on management and planning. But the functions of management and the functions of leadership are different. A project manager is usually appointed with the remit of chairing project team meetings, issuing minutes, ensuring that project plans are developed and monitoring progress and identifying issues for resolution. These activities are all very important and necessary to the management of projects, but leadership is more than these things.

Leadership is about enabling the project team to undertake excellent work, to solve problems quickly and imaginatively and continually seeking to improve ways of working. The ability of the project leader to enable the team members to really work together cross-functionally, involving the right people at the right time, to think outside the box and get away from functional silos is a skill which can really make a difference to the achievement of the team.

The project leader is responsible for delivering the project business objectives or timely termination of the project where the target or minimal acceptable product profile cannot be achieved. In order for the objectives to be met in the most timely and cost-effective manner, the leader has to create an environment in which the project team can be successful.

The traditional or "textbook definition" of a project manager's role is "the delivery of the business objectives to an appropriate quality, on time and within cost". What I am proposing here is not inconsistent with this traditional definition; I am merely expanding on how to achieve this end in the context of pharmaceutical product development. The concepts of "on time" and "to appropriate quality" are highly complex in the context of New Chemical Entity (NCE) development.

Since development projects in the pharmaceutical industry are rarely allocated a budget which is managed by the project manager, project budgeting will not be covered in this book.

The role of project leader encompasses all of the following functions:

- Leadership
- Orgánisation

- Problem solving
- Challenge
- Planning
- Monitoring and control
- Resource management
- Progress reporting
- Communication
- Upward management

A high level of management competencies is required in the individual at about that of a function or senior department head in a line management role. Additionally, it should be recognised that the management of a team spanning 30 or 40 different departments at different geographic locations in a matrix organisation will require competencies over and above those of many line management roles. Particularly, the different areas in which judgement is required to be exercised is more demanding in a broad matrix role than a more narrow line role.

The most critical competencies for an effective project leader are leadership, problem solving and teamwork. In terms of problem solving, the project leader needs the ability to lead team members in problem-solving sessions or must ensure that another team member can and is doing it, depending on the issues at the time.

The subject of resource management has been covered, it is the responsibility of the project leader to ensure that the manpower resources required for the project are identified and secured from the line manager. Line managers should ensure that agreed resources are made available as required and monitor actual allocations.

Functions of the Project Leader

A number of functions which the project leader has to fulfil—i.e., leadership, organisation, problem solving, challenge, planning, monitoring and control, progress reporting, communication and upward management—were identified above. Project planning, monitoring and control and progress reporting will be covered in later chapters; leadership has already been discussed, but it is appropriate to deal with challenge and upward management here.

Challenge

The first level of challenge to the content of project strategies and plans is a function of the project team. The project leader must ensure that

- project strategies are developed and consistent with business objectives;
- project plans are consistent with agreed strategies and objectives;
- the needs of all functions are being considered—for instance, if marketing identifies an important competitor product, clinical plans should include appropriate comparator studies;
- acceptance criteria are defined for all major milestones in the project;
- the team is seeking ways of working which will minimise the time required to complete and report studies on the critical path;
- the target profile is well developed, comprehensive and based on input from all appropriate functions; and
- competitive advantage is considered and maximised.

Upward Management

The project leader provides an interface for the team with senior management of research and development (R&D) and the business. The management team should provide broad direction, resources and priorities to the team but should avoid micro management. A good project leader will ensure that the senior R&D managers add value to the work of the project team, by getting involved only at project decision points or whenever replanning or a change of project scope is required. I have seen effective senior management teams and others that took decisions which should have been taken by the project team but without the knowledge or data required. I have seen senior R&D managers design clinical studies, determine formulations and decide regulatory strategies, yet bad decisions were taken.

A good project leader will ensure that when issues and problems are encountered in a project, the team very quickly undertakes an analysis of the problem and identifies one or more strategies for resolution. If it is not possible to identify the solution immediately, plans should be prepared, possibly with different scenarios, and decision points should be clearly identified along with time-scales. The leader must be able to clearly and simply explain the issues and the scenarios for resolution and gain the confidence of the management team. Senior managers will be less likely to get involved in the project details even when there are issues if the project team can demonstrate that it has control.

I have heard project team members discussing why certain information on project progress should be withheld from senior managers because they do not trust the management team to handle the information. These situations have lead to slippages in the project being concealed from the senior team or positive results being withheld until the project team has worked out what steps it wants to take next. Is this a reflection on the project team, its leader, the senior managers or all of the above?

Qualities of the Project Leader

Often, individuals are appointed who lack some or even many of the essential personal characteristics of the effective project leader. Also, companies do not always have personal development plans in place which allow those individuals with the right potential to be identified and developed for these important roles. This issue will be discussed further when we look at the development of project leaders.

The effective project leader will have the following personal characteristics:

- Charisma
- Intelligence
- Integrity
- Adaptability
- Decision-making capability
- Breadth and depth of experience
- Breadth of vision
- Good judgement
- Problem-solving capability
- Open-minded
- Energetic
- Proactive
- Good communication skills
- Empathetic
- Prepared to take risks
- Good organiser
- Facilitator
- Stays calm under pressure

Charisma

To be effective, the individual will have to be influential at all levels in the organisation, and possession of personal charisma is an extremely valuable asset. It is difficult to assess, but people who are self-confident, charming, interesting, good fun and likeable (a sense of humour should be compulsory), persuasive, enthusiastic and energetic will be best equipped to lead and motivate teams. The ability to elicit commitment to the project and to overcome the inevitable difficulties is also important.

Intelligence

The project leader must be able to analyse situations accurately and identify the big issues. The individual must be able to deal with large quantities of information and to simplify problems which have the potential of becoming complex. The capability to evaluate risk and deal with uncertainty is also important.

Integrity

A spirit of openness and honesty must be achieved within the project team if problems and issues are to be identified and resolved as early as possible. This trust must begin with the leader who should set standards of behaviour at the beginning of the project. The leader should be loyal to the team members, honouring his or her own commitments if commitment is to be gained in return. In particular, credit should be given where it is due.

Breadth and Depth of Experience

The project leader must understand the business and have or be prepared to gain some knowledge of the therapeutic area in which the development project is positioned. There are many times when judgement will have to be exercised in different situations, for example, in assessing priorities between conflicting requirements, knowing when additional skills and resources need to be brought into the team to solve a particular problem, and so on.

Good Judgement

Good judgement is difficult to assess, but breadth of experience and business understanding go a long way in equipping an individual with the ability to be successful in this respect. The best project leaders have had line management experience at middle management level and have professional experience in more than one area. Having lived and worked in more than one country is also beneficial in the management of international teams.

Adaptability

The ability to adapt quickly to changes in the business or regulatory environment is important, and project plans should be adapted accordingly if necessary.

Decision-Making Capability

The project leader does not and should not take all project decisions, but a leader who can take decisions will ensure that when required decisions are taken in a timely manner, delays to project time-scales are minimised.

Breadth of Vision

Strategic thinking, the ability to see the big picture and make links between various aspects of the project rather than taking a task-focussed approach is required. The ability to understand the detail and see how it fits into the big picture is necessary, as is the ability to operate at different levels. Knowing when to get involved with the detail and to what extent is a key skill. A project leader needs helicopter vision in addition to the ability to handle complex detail at times.

Problem-Solving Capability

The ability to analyse and assess situations, predict issues and problems and plan corrective actions is a key skill requirement. On occasion, completely unexpected results may be obtained, and the appropriate members of the project team need to understand the implications of the results and what action to take as a consequence.

The project leader does not have to be able to solve technical problems personally but must have the tools and skill to lead problem-solving sessions, facilitating the appropriate team members to identify all of the implications and explore all of the appropriate courses of action. The exploration of all aspects of a situation before closing down too quickly on a solution can improve the probability of success dramatically. The use of tools such as brainstorming, fault tree analysis and process mapping should be standards in the effective project leader's tool kit.

Energetic

High energy levels and enthusiasm are important for the inspiration of others, getting things done and being able to cope with the breadth of the job. Long hours and a lot of travel can be involved, and the individual must have a good level of resilience.

Proactive

If drug development times are to be minimised, the project team needs to be constantly reviewing progress and forecasting potential knock-on effects and implications for the project plan. The project leader must be very active in this area, and a proactive approach to the identification of corrective actions and their implementation is essential.

Good Communication Skills

Good communication skills are essential because the project leader has to operate at all levels in the company, the ability to communicate accurately and in a timely manner is a key to success. The ability to explain complex issues simply and to cut out unnecessary clutter is also a key skill, particularly in upward management.

Within the project team, listening skills are also very important. When ideas are rejected, the reasons why must be clearly understood. It is not enough just to listen, a project leader must be seen to be listening.

Empathetic

The ability to empathise with team members and line managers is important in getting things done and in problem solving. A readiness to understand constraints and issues that impact the ability of team members to deliver project activities or issues that impact resource availability are important. Demonstrating an understanding of the issues in addition to a willingness to work with the appropriate individuals to resolve them with minimum impact on the project is a key skill, which can make a significant difference. A project leader who always shows impatience and frustration when issues or delays arise can lose the support of team members and department managers.

The American culture is often short of empathy. Too frequently I have seen instances of leaders getting impatient or even angry. Frustration is often displayed in front of team members or line managers, and these individuals do not realise how this aggressive behaviour dilutes their power and influence. Calm, collected discussion of the issues and replacement of aggression with a true understanding of the situation and some problem solving skills are far more powerful tools to be employed.

On being told of an unpleasant encounter with a project manager, which one of my line managers experienced while working for me in a U.S. organisation, I advised the individual in the future to refuse to continue with such a discussion and to ask the project manager to leave the office. The project manager was demanding action on his project in a most inappropriate way, screaming that the lack of progress was unacceptable. At that time, the line manager was very short staffed, and delays in some tasks were unavoidable. In order to get the project manager out of the office, commitments were made which should not have been made, resources were diverted from a more important task which caused worse problems later on. As it turned out, the original project activity was not on the critical path, and the proposed delay would not have had an impact on project completion.

Unfortunately, this type of incident is not uncommon in many organisations and is a major cause of fractured relationships and poor teamwork. Aggressive behaviour on behalf of a project leader (however great the provocation) is a failure. Good team members will point this out objectively and impartially.

Facilitator

Bringing the individuals in project teams together and forming a close team that supports and trusts each other is something that the leader must achieve early in the project's life. The ability to smooth out disagreements and expedite consensus and agreement is important. A good facilitator will move project teams forward in planning, problem solving and the execution of activities.

Good Organiser

Project leadership requires a high level of organisational skills to plan, arrange and manage meetings; collect information for planning and monitoring purposes; and produce timely and relevant progress reports.

In addition to these personal characteristics, the project leader must have authority vested in him or her by the organisation, in terms of the personal reporting relationship and the degree of support afforded to the position by the president and vice presidents of R&D. The reporting relationship should be to the most senior person possible, preferably directly to a senior vice president or president of R&D.

SHOULD PROJECT LEADERS BE FULL–TIME PROFESSIONALS?

Historically, some companies have employed full-time project leaders at a very senior level, but it is more common to employ full-time project managers at a more junior level. If project leaders are appointed, they are line managers who support the project manager.

Full-time project managers, however, tend to have a brief that is more focussed on management rather than leadership. The emphasis tends to be on planning, organising meetings, providing management information and progress chasing.

The case for full-time, high-calibre project leaders is strong for projects in the regulatory phase of development, certainly from Phase 2 onward for compounds that the company has decided to fast track.

There is a case for managing exploratory development projects differently from regulatory phase projects, particularly in those companies that employ full-time project directors at a senior level. At the early stages of development, project teams are smaller, reflecting the fact that the scope of the project is smaller with respect to the number of departments involved.

The following are advantages for having full-time project leaders:

- Provides an opportunity to appoint a senior individual with broad experience, bringing high-level management skills to the team and being dedicated to the project on a full-time basis.
- Sends a message to the project team and their line managers that the project is of strategic importance to the company.
- Brings knowledge about the functioning of the company and knows how to get things done.
- Facilitates learning within the cadre of project leaders.

Yet there is also a disadvantage to having a full-time project leader: It may be difficult to recruit sufficient individuals with the experience and personal qualities described above.

ALTERNATIVES TO PROJECT LEADERS

Full-Time Project Managers

Full-time project managers are more junior in the organisation, may not have all of the personal characteristics and will not have extensive business experience. Such a scenario has three advantages:

1. It is easier to recruit suitable individuals.
2. It is one way to develop individuals into project leader positions.
3. It is appropriate for line extension projects rather than NCEs.

Project Leader with Support from Project Manager

Another alternative to the full-time project leader is the appointment of a project leader who is a senior line manager with support from a full-time project manager. This scenario has two advantages:

1. Senior line managers will bring the management experience and many of the personal characteristics described for the project leader.
2. Provides more flexibility as the number of projects in regulatory development change.

However, there are disadvantages for the organisation with this approach.

- It is difficult for a manager to do two jobs—either the project will get less attention than is required or the line function will suffer.
- The opportunity to learn from previous projects will be diminished.

DEVELOPMENT OF PROJECT LEADERS

I mentioned earlier that many companies do not make enough of this strategically important role. There are many reasons for this: the reluctance of traditional pharmaceutical companies to really embrace matrix management, the reluctance to change from management systems which have been successful in the past and, significantly, the scarcity of individuals with the breadth of experience and personal qualities to undertake these roles.

Many biotech and other small entrepreneurial companies are exploiting matrix management, and the role of the project leader is a senior one often reporting to a member of the board. These companies have recognised the advantage that high-performing project teams can bring to the development process.

The search for ways of reducing time to market and improved productivity in R&D is, however, causing even the more traditional companies to re-examine their project management systems. The need to redefine the role of the project manager or project leader, and the skills and qualities of individuals in these roles, is also recognised by many. However, few companies are positively developing individuals into these positions, which is a serious omission in their manpower planning strategies. A proactive development programme that identifies young talented scientific managers who are interested in a career in management and provides them with opportunities to gain broader experience in the business and management training is the key to success in this area.

So what should a development plan for project leaders look like? Clearly, there are a number of skills that can be obtained from training courses, and I will discuss these later, but the most important part of the development plan should be on broadening the business experience base of the individual. This part of the plan will depend to a great extent on where the individual starts from in his or her early career. Project leaders can come from almost anywhere in the business, but it is likely that they will start in R&D or on the interface such as strategic marketing, industrialisation or within a medical or regulatory function in an operating company that is not part of core R&D.

For individuals who start their careers in R&D, a period of time spent in an operating company will add a different dimension to their experience. Any position which brings some commercial awareness of the business will be of enormous value later on. A period of time working in another country will also be very beneficial, particularly if it involves having to learn another language and learning to become effective in another culture.

The ability to deal with conflict and cross-cultural behaviour will stand any prospective senior manager, be it in a line or matrix role, in extremely good stead. Americans, Europeans and the Japanese all have different styles and preferred ways of working with respect to sharing information and decision making. Understanding these differences is an important issue to the leader of a cross-functional, multinational team.

In terms of formal training, there are a number of subject areas where courses will be useful. An MBA is a valuable, broad-based qualification which will cover most of the key subject areas;

however, training in the following can be gained in a number of ways:

- Leadership styles and attributes
- Change management
- Strategic decision making
- Team dynamics
- Influencing skills
- Economics
- Finance for non-financial managers
- Experimental design
- Statistical methods in management
- Problem solving
- Presentation skills
- Project management methods
- Planning

Many more could be added to the list, but it depends on the interests of the person concerned. In addition, the attendance at seminars and conferences which cover issues of importance to the industry, such as reducing development times, improving productivity in R&D, regulatory issues, health economics and so on, should be expected and encouraged. Again, the list is potentially long, and many conferences and seminars are held annually. Their purpose is to raise the awareness of individuals to key issues affecting the industry, which will stimulate project leaders to encourage project teams to address these aspects in the design of development programmes.

The benefit to the organisation from investment in the development of highly skilled project leaders will be much greater productivity in development programmes. A broad awareness of the business and issues of strategic importance to the company will make the project leader more effective in ensuring that the cross-functional aspects of the development programme are addressed. This is not a strength of many line managers, who tend to be specialists in one or two fields but have less appreciation of the wider business issues. The role of the management team described in Chapter 3 is to ensure that all of the business issues are addressed by challenging the project plans; however, the more comprehensive the plan, the less the likelihood of issues being missed during the challenge process.

Very large project teams are inefficient and largely ineffective. Getting the project team structure, composition and ways of working right are major challenges for most companies.

I have seen project team meetings attended by as many as 30 people. Agendas have moved from planning to problem solving to information exchange (e.g., numbers of doses required for a clinical trial discussed after long discussions on the objective of drug interaction studies, followed by an update of the high-level project plan). These meetings can take several hours, and some attendees make no specific contribution; their attendance was motivated merely to find out what is going on a certain aspect of interest. These large, unstructured meetings rarely accomplish as much as the number of man-hours invested should realise.

If the project team is structured correctly and communication of progress is appropriate, team meetings can be more effective and less time-consuming for the team members. Effective team meetings have only one or two objectives and will fall into one of the following categories:

- Planning
- Problem solving
- Progress reporting/information exchange

The composition of the project team must reflect the scope of the organisation in terms of its international nature, and skills must be appropriate to the project.

•

My preference for the project structure is one composed of a core project team lead by a senior individual, each core team member is effectively a leader of a project subteam. In this way, the full project team meetings can be used as a vehicle for high-level planning, cross-functional progress reporting and information exchange. The subteams can then become the vehicle for detailed planning and problem resolution.

The project team should be international and reflect the nature of the organisation. Roles and responsibilities should be defined and agreed on for each member of the core project team; similarly, roles and responsibilities for members of the subteams should also be defined.

The composition of the team and probably its leader will change through the lifetime of the project. Exploratory development will require significant input from preclinical safety, pharmacokinetics, drug metabolism and clinical pharmacology. Regulatory phase development will require significant input from therapeutic research, marketing, industrialisation and regulatory departments.

The composition of the team and its structure should be reviewed when a project moves from exploratory development to regulatory development, and the leadership of subteams may also need to change at certain times. For example, the leadership of the chemical process development and pharmaceutical process development teams may change as the processes are scaled up and transferred to manufacturing. Leadership of the clinical development team may need to change between Phase 2 and Phase 3 programmes according to the geographic spread of the pivotal studies.

In international organisations, it is very important to ensure that the project team includes the correct representatives from key functions. The regulatory, clinical development and marketing teams must have representatives from the U.S., European and Japanese arms of the business if the project plans are to reflect global requirements.

11

Effective Project Teams and Team Structures

To be highly effective, project teams must be appropriately structured and led. The culture should foster innovation and creativity as well as cross-functional teamwork.

There are many different possible team structures, but in this chapter I will propose a structure which from experience is the most effective in an international pharmaceutical company.

ATTRIBUTES OF HIGHLY EFFECTIVE PROJECT TEAMS

The following attributes apply to highly effective project teams (Figure 11.1):

- Right size—not too large
- Highly effective leader

Figure 11.1. Effective Project Teams

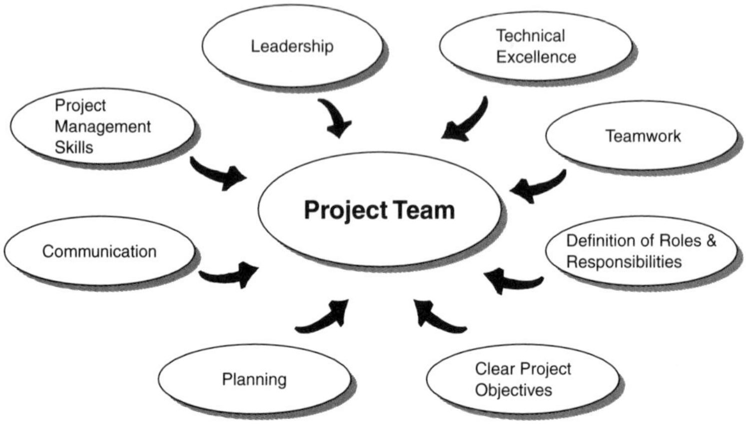

- Appropriate membership
- Appropriate scientific expertise
- Good teamwork skills
- Clearly defined roles and responsibilities
- Empowered
- Highly motivated
- Results oriented
- Committed

Some of these attributes are discussed in more detail below.

Right Size

Teams with more than 8 to 10 members cannot function as a single team, freely interacting with each other, raising issues and solving problems. If teams become too large, they tend to break up into subgroups or just fail to function as a coherent team with a single identity. From the nomination of a compound for development to product launch, a development project will require input from between 30 to 50 different departments, depending on the size and structure of the company. If working teams are to be kept small, the project team should be structured to form small operating units, which can develop an identity and become high-performance teams.

Highly Effective Leader

We have already looked at the personal characteristics of the project leader (Chapter 10) and saw that leadership is one of the most important roles. The project leader's role in the effective project team is to provide the following:

- *Set direction:*
  - Set and achieve approval of a clear set of project objectives.
  - Define the project team with appropriate membership and structure.
  - Develop the project strategy and decision criteria.
  - Develop a written project plan at the right level of detail.
  - Define acceptance criteria for major milestones.
  - Agree on performance targets.
- *Develop and build the team:*
  - Form a team identity for the core project team and subteams.
  - Develop ownership of the project objectives and plan within the team.
  - Secure the resources required to deliver the project.
  - Give recognition of achievements.
  - Facilitate problem solving.
- *Provide inspiration:*
  - Inspire project team members to perform at their very best.

- Sponsor continuous improvement in ways of working to reduce project lead times.
- Be a champion for the team within the organisation.

The effective leader coaches the team and achieves the above through the involvement of all its members. In this way, the team owns the plan and the performance targets, not the project leader, which is a critical success factor for the highly effective team.

Appropriate Membership and Scientific Expertise

Assignment of the right individuals to a project team is fundamental to its success. Each team member must be of sufficient calibre to contribute to the development of strategies and plans and to make decisions on behalf of the department to which he or she belongs. Since the members of the core project team must lead subteams, the individuals must have leadership skills and be of sufficient seniority to manage critical elements of the project. Any weak links in the core team will compromise the success of elements of the project and must be corrected.

Good Teamwork Skills

The team members need to have a high level of teamwork skills. In addition to their own scientific expertise, the individuals must bring the following attributes to the project:

- Understand how drug development is done.
- Support other team members.
- Contribute to problem solving.
- Challenge plans and study designs to promote excellence.
- Capable of taking decisions.
- Represent their department managers in the commitment of resources.

- Honour commitments made to the team.
- Does not undermine the team outside the project.
- Communicate effectively on progress in own area.
- Be open and frank.
- Be self-disciplined.
- Set values and standards of behaviour for the team and implement them.

Empowered

An effective team is one that is empowered to do a job. Once the right individuals have been assigned to the project team, they must have the support of research and development (R&D) management to get on with planning and implementing the project activities.

In order to move projects forward, team members must have the right skills and competencies. There is no value in empowering individuals who do not have the necessary expertise; such empowerment will produce disappointing results. Everyone knows the scene of an individual rearranging deck chairs on the *Titanic* as it sunk. Empowerment of individuals who do not have the correct skills will result in overemphasis of trivial details and a failure to address the most important issues.

Department managers and function heads should provide guidance when needed, challenge plans and so on, but they must not undermine the project team by trying to its job.

Committed

Given the right membership, empowerment from the senior management team and a good project leader, commitment in the project team should be high. Commitment is obtained through involvement, and once a clear direction is set, the project team will develop plans and strategies that its members will be keen to implement. The right team members set high standards and are prepared to work diligently to meet them.

Membership of the team for projects in Phase 2 and beyond should ideally be a full-time commitment for certain members of the clinical research team; there should be no other competing priorities. In other departments, it may not be possible or necessary for team members to be dedicated full time. However, all team members should feel comfortable with what they are expected to deliver and have the time and resources to deliver it. The relationship with the project leader is an important one in this regard; he or she must ensure that the environment is one that will promote success.

Teams deserve credit for achievements, and they should celebrate successes when overcoming difficult technical challenges or meeting tight deadlines. Newsletters, bulletin board notices reporting achievements of major milestones and road shows are not only good communication tools for the business but also are highly motivating for the project team. Out of hours social activities are also important, particularly at the initiation of projects when the team is still forming. These help the team form a cohesive bond.

A leader cannot motivate a team member—motivation is a personal thing that comes from within. A good leader can create an environment where motivated individuals can perform. The actions of a poor leader, however, can reduce an individual's level of motivation and the personal desire to give of his or her best.

Results Oriented

The effective project team develops realistic plans and sets clear deliverables for each milestone. The project plan is directed to the achievement of results and hitting milestones, providing good quality data on which decisions can be made. Encouraged to innovate and monitor their own performance, the team will find ways of reducing lead-times and delivering high quality work.

TYPICAL TEAM STRUCTURES

Exploratory Development

Exploratory development or Phase 1 is less complicated to manage than later stage development, and a single team is probably all that is required. In addition to the project leader, team members will typically consist of individuals from the following departments:

- Process Chemistry
- Preclinical Safety
- Pharmaceutical Sciences
- Clinical Pharmacology
- Marketing
- Analytical Chemistry
- Pharmacology
- Regulatory Affairs

The role of the team is to develop a detailed plan to the end of Phase 1, including acceptance criteria, especially the definition of safety criteria and the clinical endpoint. An outline plan to launch identifying possible target indications will be helpful in decision making around safety issues and the design of Phase 1 clinical studies. The management team and appropriate direction given to the project team for implementation should decide the strategy of fastest track to first exposure in humans versus early commitment to a more comprehensive toxicology programme.

Regulatory Development—Phase 2 Onward

For development beyond Phase 2, the membership will change somewhat. It is at this stage where the appointment of a high calibre project leader is most appropriate. Since the number of individuals working on the project will increase substantially, a more formal team structure consisting of a core team (Figure 11.2) and cross-functional subteams is the most effective organisation. Each member of the core team and the subteams must have clearly defined roles and responsibilities, which should be included in the written project plan (see Chapter 2).

It is most important that the core team be composed of senior individuals from the following departments:

- Clinical Development
- Safety Evaluation
- Pharmaceutical Sciences
- Process Chemistry
- Regulatory Affairs
- Marketing
- Industrialisation

Figure 11.2. The Core Project Team

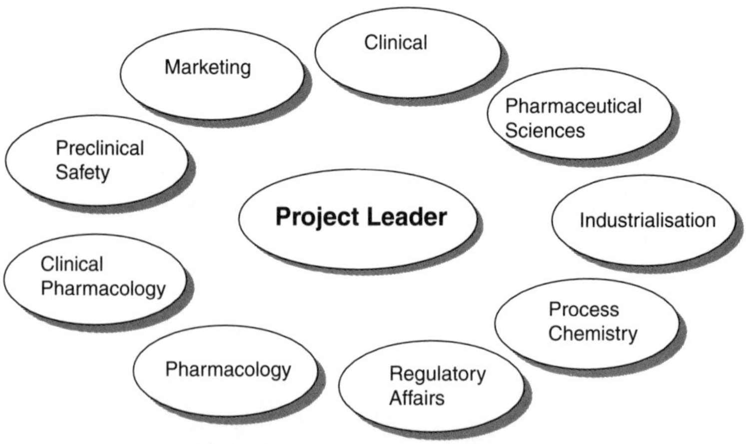

The Role of the Core Project Team

It is the role of the core project team to undertake the following:

- Develop project strategies in line with guidance from the management team.
- Develop project plans.
- Define acceptance criteria for each major milestone.
- Monitor and control progress against the plan.
- Raise issues and solve problems.
- Develop contingency plans.

Project Subteams

Project subteams composed along the lines of the work to be undertaken (consistent with the project work breakdown structure) is one way to improve the productivity of the project team. These subteams will be cross-functional but will focus on a subset of project activities, such as the clinical programme, process development, technology transfer and so on. Typical memberships of subteams are given below.

Clinical Development

The clinical development team will itself be cross-functional and led by the person responsible for the clinical programme, usually a physician from central R&D. The following members are typically included:

- Physicians running subprogrammes (corporate and affiliate representatives)
- Clinical research associates (CRAs) running the studies
- Statisticians
- A representative from Clinical Trial Supplies

- Regulatory affairs specialist
- Marketing professional
- A pharmacologist or clinical pharmacologist
- A medical writer

The role of this team is as follows:

- Develop clinical development objectives in line with agreed-on project strategy and market requirements.
- Develop clinical plans consistent with project objectives.
- Develop acceptance criteria for major milestones.
- Work with opinion leaders to develop an interest in the drug.
- Implement the clinical plan.
- Monitor team performance and implement improved ways of working where possible.
- Provide input to the training of sales forces.
- Provide regulatory documents.
- Ensure publications are produced in a timely manner.

It is usual for studies to be set up in the United States, Europe and Japan, and the physicians running each part of the programme should all be members of the clinical development team. This will ensure that study designs will be consistent and monitored to the same standards of Good Clinical Practice (GCP), and the number of patients entered into the studies can be kept to a minimum without compromising the power of the studies. The CRAs running the studies should also be members of the team. Experiences can be exchanged, and any problems with the design of diary cards or case report forms can be identified early and rectified; feedback from statisticians on data entered on the first patients to complete the study can be valuable in ironing out any issues. Early feedback from clinicians on patient entry criteria, patient compliance and so on can also be very useful in correcting problems. If the CRAs remain close to each other and exchange all information available in a timely manner, the quality of the data ultimately produced from the clinical trials will be much better than if the CRAs work in isolation.

This type of team formation is, in practice, not encouraged. I have experienced situations where there have been major disagreements between the members of U.S. and European clinical development teams so much that study designs became so different that the results could not be combined.

The formation of a team involving physicians and CRAs from the U.S. and European arms of the organisation takes a lot of skill. Agreeing on a set of common objectives and study designs is not an easy task because the markets are different. A decision has to be made as to whether the European and U.S. arms of a clinical development programme should be of the same design. Clearly, it is only appropriate for the studies to be designed in the same way if the product is the same.

Even if the product design and study designs are different, there are still significant benefits to be obtained in sharing information generated on the product, particularly as the time-scales for starting the studies are often different. CRAs running later-starting studies can be better prepared if they have information from earlier-starting studies.

Preclinical Safety

The preclinical safety team will be led by the toxicologist responsible for the programme and typically will have the following membership:

- Toxicologists responsible for the individual studies
- A histopathologist
- A clinical pathologist
- A drug metabolist
- An analyst

- A bioanalyst
- A pharmacokineticist
- Possibly a pharmacologist
- A quality assurance (QA) specialist

This team is responsible for planning and implementing all of the preclinical safety studies. These plans need to include forecasts of drug requirements and the availability of resources, including animals and the management of contract houses.

Good cross-functional communication is essential. The "isolation" of animal laboratories from other development functions can prove to be a challenge for this team.

I have experienced situations where the toxicologists have not communicated adequately with the members of process chemistry regarding drug substance quantities and the analysis of samples by the analytical laboratory. Project delays have been incurred as a result.

It is also very important to have one person responsible for the study schedule. This person will ensure that all other departments, including QA or the function responsible for the GLP (Good Laboratory Practice) audit of reports, know when support activities need to begin, when samples will be available and when reports will be available for review. Most analytical chemistry departments do not have crystal balls, but many are criticised for poor turnaround of results on samples that they were unaware of until they appeared, often inappropriately labelled, from an anonymous study director.

The role of this team is to

- develop objectives for the toxicology programme;
- develop acceptance criteria for each milestone in the plan;
- develop the toxicology study plan;
- secure all resources including people, materials and animals;

- undertake studies;
- advise and support the clinical development team on the basis of study findings; and
- provide regulatory reports and expert statements.

Pharmaceutical Sciences

The pharmaceutical sciences team will be led initially by the formulation pharmacist, but it is appropriate for the leadership to change as technology transfer and scale-up into production take place. The leader at the scale-up stage is appropriately the person responsible for transfer, scale-up and process validation. Typically, the team will consist of the following members:

- A formulation pharmacist
- A pre-formulation pharmacist
- A process development pharmacist
- A packaging technologist
- An analytical chemist
- A marketing product manager
- An industrialisation member
- A regulatory affairs officer

The above constitutes the core team, and inputs from the following departments will be required from time to time at critical points in the development programme:

- The physician responsible for the clinical programme
- Clinical Trial Supplies
- Toxicology
- Quality Assurance

- Purchasing
- External consultants as required

This is a long list of departments and represents a large team. It is not necessary for the entire team to meet on a frequent basis, and most meetings will be of subgroups who will meet to plan, discuss issues and resolve technical problems. It is useful for the core team to meet on a regular basis to communicate and to monitor progress against the function plan. All individuals must have defined roles, and the inclusion of members from other departments will facilitate timely scheduling of activities in support functions, and team members will know who their contacts are.

Pharmaceutical Development

The role of the pharmaceutical development team is as follows:

- Design the product in line with clinical, regulatory and marketing requirements.
- Specify product performance and develop acceptance criteria.
- Design and develop the manufacturing process.
- Select appropriate technology.
- Specify process performance and acceptance criteria for clinical trials manufacturing.
- Select primary and secondary packaging.
- Determine product shelf life.
- Develop product and packaging specifications.
- Select and approve material and equipment suppliers in line with approved company supplier policy.
- Develop contingency plans.
- Provide clinical trial and stability programme supplies.

- Provide regulatory documentation.
- Develop project plans.

Process Chemistry

Typical team members on the process chemistry team will include representatives from the following departments:

- Process development team leader
- A process chemist from Industrialisation
- Team leader from Analytical Chemistry
- Clinical Trial Supplies
- Physical Chemistry
- Pre-formulation
- Quality Assurance
- Purchasing
- Representative from Contract Manufacturer (as appropriate)
- Regulatory Affairs
- Health and Safety

If any or all of the stages of synthesis are contracted out, then it is important that the contract manufacturer's process development chemists are included on the team for issues concerning their stage of the synthesis. The exchange of planning and scheduling information must be good, and the contract manufacturer must be clear as to what the deliverables are, and when quantities of the compound are required. Conversely, if problems occur, the process team should be involved in problem solving and be flexible enough to change activities accordingly. The team must strike the right balance between utilisation of the contract manufacturer's expertise and facilities and control of the programme to quality time and cost targets.

Process Development

The role of the process development team is as follows:

- Design the synthetic route.
- Specify performance criteria.
- Develop the project plan.
- Design, develop and validate the process.
- Develop specifications for intermediates and bulk pharmaceutical chemicals (BPCs).
- Provide quantities of BPCs to support development activities.
- Provide clinical trial supplies.
- Manage contract manufacturers.
- Identify safety issues and provide safe handling procedures.

Regulatory Affairs

The regulatory affairs team should ensure that all key requirements are identified and integrated into the development plan. Therefore, team members will include regulatory experts from the United States, Europe and Japan. While it is recognised that Japanese requirements are different from those of the U.S. Food and Drug Administration (FDA) and European authorities, it is not necessary to run two complete development programmes.

Much of the toxicology programme can fulfil international needs by paying attention to the number of animals in the studies and the treatment times and doses. Careful planning of these studies, which will require some modification to purely FDA or European guidelines, can avoid having to repeat major studies for Japanese protocols. This approach has two major benefits:

1. The overall cost of the toxicology programme will be less by implementing combined protocols than running two parallel programmes.

2. Time-scales for the Japanese programme can be reduced, resulting in earlier launches in this major market.

The role of the regulatory affairs team is as follows:

- Develop the regulatory strategy.
- Support the project team in the identification and interpretation of regulatory requirements for each major element in the development plan.
- Obtain Investigational New Drug (IND), Clinical Trial Exemption (CTX) and other approvals for clinical studies.
- Seek advice from the FDA and other regulatory bodies on difficult project issues and major study designs.
- Build good working relationships with key regulatory authorities.
- Compile and submit dossiers.

Marketing

The constitution of the marketing team, which can reflect the views of the major markets and integrate them in the development plan, will be most effective for the business. There are four areas where marketing input is clearly essential:

1. Early development—input to target profile and minimum acceptable profile, product design and clinical indication
2. Provision of market forecasts for capacity planning and site selection
3. Development of the marketing strategy, launch platform and pre-launch activities
4. Definition of publications to support launches

There is a tendency for headquarters marketing staff to have input into development plans, particularly in Phase 1 and 2 when the products are outside the operational planning horizons, and when the probability of the product ever reaching the market is still relatively low. This is understandable and logical, but it is in the long-term interests of the project to ensure that the views of key markets are obtained as early as possible, when decisions on product design and clinical indications are being made. Getting it right at this stage is important to the long-term success of the product. It is the job of the marketing member on the core project team to establish early contacts with colleagues in the operating companies and to ensure that there is good two-way feedback on these critical issues.

Good quality feedback cannot be obtained from the markets unless good quality information on options and alternatives being considered by the project team are provided for consideration and comment. Whether this communication is via individuals in the operating companies allocated to the project formally or whether it is effected by road shows and regular contact with product managers or marketing directors is a matter of choice and depends on the size and structure of the company. I raise it here as a team structure issue only to emphasise the importance of getting the right level of input early in the project.

Operating company input to pre-launch activities can be obtained very successfully by the team approach, although it may be advantageous to form regional teams (i.e., the United States, Europe, Asia and Pacific, emerging markets, etc.). Operating company input at late Phase 3 or even Phase 4 is far too late and, in my experience, leads to less successful launches than products deserve and creeping product ranges. The greatest benefit to including operating companies early in the development of the launch platform will be their input into the design of Phase 3B or Phase 4 marketing studies. The operating companies will be best placed to understand what the opinion leaders want to know concerning relative performance to existing therapies and so on.

The role of the marketing team is as follows:

- Understand the market for the therapeutic area.
- Be familiar with the competition and keep up to date with developments.

- Be familiar with and keep up to date with opinion leaders and views.
- Be familiar with corporate business strategies and maintain links with operating companies.
- Develop a marketing strategy for the development project.
- Contribute to the development of the target and minimal acceptable product profile to ensure good product positioning and differentiation.
- Provide sales projections for each indication and dosage form.
- Provide input to the product design.
- Provide input to acceptance criteria for go/no go decisions.
- Secure successful product launches in major territories.
- Provide input to clinical development plans.
- Develop launch strategies.
- Build good relationships with clinical opinion leaders.
- Provide input to trademarks.
- Determine pricing policy.
- Work with clinical development and preclinical departments to secure publications.
- Provide training for sales forces.
- Organise launch activities (conferences, etc.).
- Input to product labelling.

The best definition I have seen of the role of marketing in an organisation is to "harmonise the organisation with its environment". This requires an intimate knowledge of the company, its products and the target markets; a good knowledge of the competition; and familiarity with the therapeutic area.

It is essential that the marketing team members understand the needs of the major world markets—U.S., European Union, Japan, Africa and Asia. Wherever possible, harmonisation of packaging, trademarks and so on is very valuable, but profit maximisation should be a major objective of this team.

In my past role as a project leader, I wanted the marketing representatives to seek and provide input from the sales and marketing functions of all major company affiliates. However, I often found that project team members from the Corporate Marketing Department would provide input that was directly at odds with the views of sales and marketing staff in even the most important of the company affiliates. These differences would range from package size, packaging, product image and pricing policy to launch strategies. Some of these differences then resulted in delays to projects. For example, changes requested in primary and secondary packaging at the last minute delay regulatory submissions due to the need for stability data on changes in primary packaging.

It is not possible to accommodate every preference from every market, but it is important to understand the main drivers in the major markets and to distinguish those requests that will have the biggest impact on the sales and profitability of the product. If differences in packaging really can affect profitability in large markets, it is not in the best interest of the company to pursue standardisation.

Early identification of different market needs will enable the project team to accommodate the requirements, with minimal impact on launch timings and the cost of goods. The cost of change (Table 11.1) increases exponentially the later in the project the changes are made, and this is particularly true for devices and novel delivery systems.

Industrialisation/Manufacturing

Industrialisation or manufacturing input (dependent on the structure of the organisation) will include both primary and secondary manufacture and may, in fact, require two teams if the primary process is being developed in-house for the first launches.

Table 11.1.
The Cost of Change

Stage	Relative Cost
Concept	1
Detail design	10
Tooling	100
Product approval and testing	1,000
Post-launch	10,000

The industrialisation team will need to be involved at the start of Phase 2 or just before depending on the product. (If primary manufacture is being undertaken in-house, the Industrialisation Department should be involved as soon as the outline route of synthesis has been chosen.) However, the initial input will be at a low level of activity, which increases as the product goes through Phase 3 and ultimately to launch.

Typically, two industrialisation teams will be required, one for the primary process and a similar team for the secondary process, since the individuals will require different experience and expertise.

The primary team will be constituted earlier in the development phase, since the process will have to be essentially developed and frozen in time to produce the drug substance for long-term toxicology studies and Phase 3 clinical supplies. The team will consist of members of the following departments:

- Primary Process Development
- Analytical Development
- Primary Manufacturing or Contract Manufacturing
- Supply Chain
- Purchasing
- Engineering
- Packaging

- Quality Assurance
- Regulatory Affairs

The secondary team will look very similar in terms of membership:

- Pharmaceutical Technology
- Analytical Development
- Secondary Manufacturing
- Supply Chain
- Purchasing
- Engineering
- Quality Assurance
- Packaging
- Regulatory Affairs

For major new product introductions, the industrialisation team will benefit from its own project manager who sits on the core project team and works with the project director to ensure that scale-up and validation of the primary and secondary processes proceed according to the overall project plan. This is particularly important if Phase 3 clinical supplies are manufactured at the site of manufacture and not in an R&D clinical trial supplies or pilot facility.

If new facilities or major modifications to existing manufacturing plants are required, then additional teams will be needed to provide these facilities. The leaders of these teams do not need to join the core project team, but they must be integrated with the industrialisation team. Here I will explain the importance of developing an appropriate team structure and integrating the industrialisation plan with the overall project plan, such that new manufacturing facilities are available to provide product in good time for launch.

Before I go into more detail about teams and plans, it is important to understand the business processes that are involved in technology transfer to manufacturing (Figure 11.3). Below I have summarised those business processes which are involved from the design of the product in development to acceptance of the process by the manufacturing site. These processes are broadly the same for both primary and secondary manufacturing.

Product development within R&D is responsible for product design and process development; product development may also be responsible for the selection of manufacturing equipment. The industrialisation team must ensure that a manufacturing strategy and a sourcing strategy are developed for the new product, early in the development process. The manufacturing strategy for the BPC should be decided during Phase 1 and for the marketed product during Phase 2. If the introduction of a new product should require any of the following, the industrialisation team must manage facilities development and validation and equipment procurement, installation and validation.

- Capacity increase in an existing manufacturing facility
- New manufacturing technology
- Modification to an existing manufacturing facility
- New manufacturing facility

If new manufacturing facilities are required, this aspect of the work is often contracted out to professional design and build companies. These companies will design the facility to the client's requirements and provide project management for the design and building of the new manufacturing facility. In such a case, the industrialisation team must ensure that the facilities team has a complete understanding of the processes which will be carried out in the facility, the equipment footprints and specifications and all environmental and services requirements for the manufacturing processes. Therefore, the industrialisation team will play a significant role in the design of the new facility. When the facilities are handed over by the design and build company, equipment installation and validation will also have to be completed

Figure 11.3. Critical Processes in Product Development and Technology Transfer

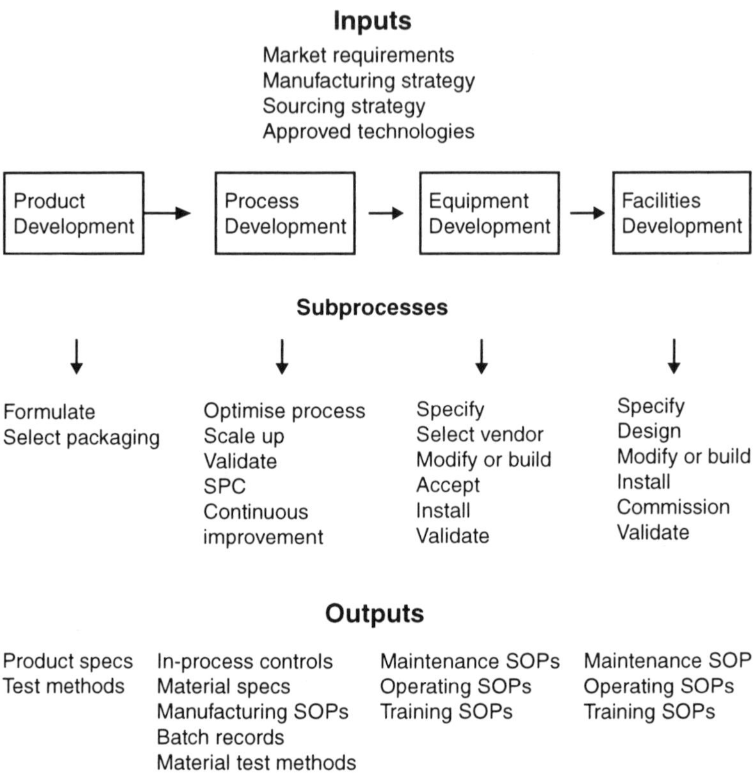

These processes do not progress sequentially; there are a lot of parrallel activities, and facilities validation precedes equipment validation, which precedes process validation

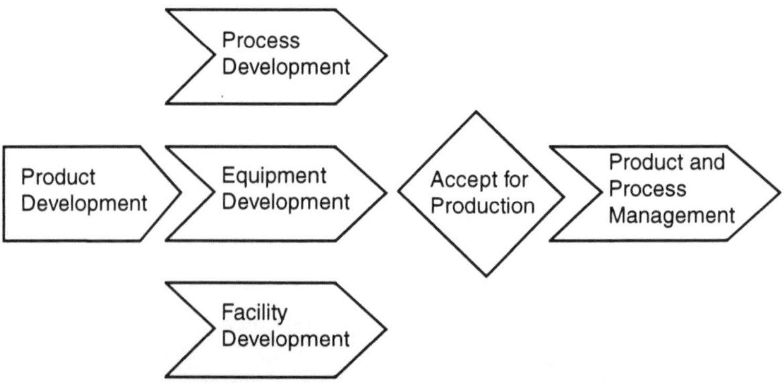

by this team. Modifications to existing facilities are often managed in-house, but the involvement of the industrialisation team will be similar: input to the design of the facility and acceptance when the modifications are completed.

The project leader of the industrialisation team can be a member of the project core team if a major facility and equipment design and development programme are planned. This project leader is responsible to the core team for delivering the manufacturing capability in time for the first product launch. This will also include the registration of the new facility, submission of Drug Master Files (DMFs), site master plans and so on.

The industrialisation project plan must include all of the following details:

- Manufacturing strategy
- Sourcing strategy for BPC, marketed product and all excipients and components
- Validation master plan
- Process description and process scale-up and validation plan
- Provision of manufacturing facility
- Manufacturing equipment procurement, installation and validation
- Definition of supply chain
- Supply contracts for active ingredients, excipients and components as required
- Supplier development and approval plans
- Manufacturing ways of working and performance measures
- Development of all manufacturing Standard Operating Procedures (SOPs)
- Manpower development and training plan for manufacturing personnel

- Cost of goods targets
- Postimplementation review

The acceptance criteria for each process must be identified in the plan so that process capability can be developed accordingly. For critical aspects of each manufacturing process, CpK values should be set at 1.33. In certain cases, this may not be achievable at the time of first launch; in such cases, the CpK should be greater than 1.0, and process controls should be implemented such that the process stays within strictly defined limits.

Acceptance criteria should also be developed for equipment performance, down time, wastage levels, batch changeover and cleaning times. Targets should be set for the entire supply chain to minimise the time from materials ordered to goods dispatched to the customer. Targets for stocks should be set and actively managed. In the product introduction phase, sufficient safety stocks should be maintained to ensure that the market can be supplied, and sensitivity analyses of the sales forecasts should be undertaken and stock levels set accordingly in agreement with the Marketing Department.

The manufacturing strategy should include a plan not only for the first launches but also for the longer-term supply. This strategy should include dual sourcing of active ingredient and pharmaceutical products or identify the levels of strategic stocks required if single sourcing is decided. Most companies will choose a single source for the first few years, since this approach simplifies technology transfer and facilitates rapid development times.

The project team structure must be developed according to the scope of each industrialisation project. Figure 11.4 shows the subteams required, but the size and scope of each one will depend on the scope of the work required. If a new product can be introduced using existing facilities and equipment, the facility subteam, for example, will be required only to ensure that the validation platform for the facility is up to date. The scope will be very different if major facilities and equipment development programmes are required.

Figure 11.4. Project Team Structures: Industrialisation Team

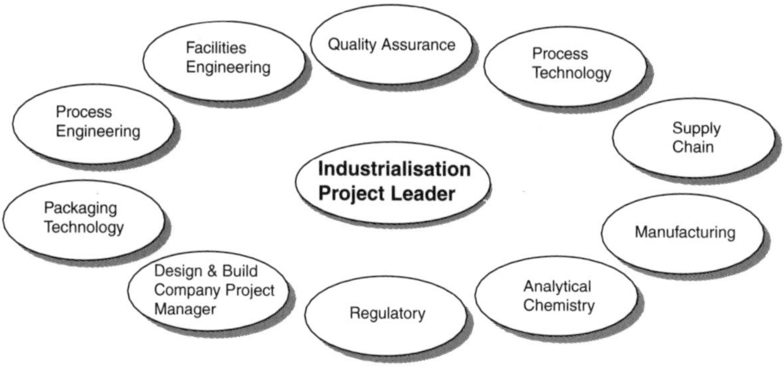

Analytical Chemistry

Analytical chemists are members of the pharmaceutical sciences and primary process development teams. However, for test method transfer, the development of a small analytical team composed of analysts from laboratories involved in the transfer will be extremely valuable.

This team must ensure that the test methods to be transferred to the Quality Control (QC) Laboratory are suitable for routine testing and validated and that the QC analysts are trained and qualified. The analytical team must provide approved specifications with supporting data and test methods for regulatory submissions. This will require input from the product design and process design teams. A member of Quality Assurance should approve final specifications and test methods.

12

Case Studies

CASE STUDY 1: DEVELOPMENT OF THE ECLIPSE INHALATION DEVICE[1]

Background

In 1994, the Montreal Protocol on the use of CFCs (chlorofluorocarbons) in manufacturing restricted CFC use in the manufacture of essential products. Certain categories of medicinal aerosols were assigned essential use status. Nonessential products could no longer use CFCs in the manufacturing process.

The pharmaceutical industry had started to search for alternative propellants for medicinal aerosols in the 1980s, but development and approval of the alternatives was a long-term exercise. In 1994, the first aerosols with alternative propellants were not expected to be available until 1996, and complete replacement of all products in all markets was not expected until 1999.

1. Presented by B. A. Lead at Management Forum, June 1998.

Since 1994, the time-scale for the introduction of many new aerosol formulations (based on HFAs [hydrofluoroalkanes]) have slipped due to the technological difficulties in manufacturing components and the formulations.

In certain Scandinavian countries, sales of aerosol products for the treatment of asthma were restricted to pre-1994 volumes, which lead the Scandinavian affiliate of the company for which I was working to request the rapid development of a new inhalation device for use with an existing capsule product. The company affiliate worked in collaboration with a local engineer who designed a capsule device that could be used with existing products. The rights to this design were obtained by the local company affiliate, and approval to develop this device in conjunction with the inventor was given by the company in July 1995.

In September 1995, I took responsibility for the Industrialisation Department, and one of my new responsibilities was the development of line extensions to support local business units. The development of this device came within my area of responsibility, and the mission was to launch in early 1997. In September 1995, the status of the project was as follows:

- An agreement had been signed with the inventor, which was his first device project for the pharmaceutical industry.
- The performance of device models met acceptance criteria.
- The inventor had selected the supplier.
- The supplier had not previously manufactured devices for the pharmaceutical industry.
- A hostile takeover bid had just been made for the company for which I worked.
- A project team had not been formally appointed for the development programme.

The first task was to form a project team and to develop strategies, objectives and plans.

Team Development

A project team was appointed to develop the device. It was composed of a small core team with members from the following areas:

- Project Champion: general manager of the local business unit
- Project Leader: director of Industrialisation
- Analytical Chemistry
- Device Engineering
- Inventor
- Clinician
- Business Development
- Marketing
- Regulatory Affairs
- Project manager

This core team was responsible for determining the development strategy, defining project objectives and acceptance criteria and developing the project plan. As the project progressed, a number of subteams were formed to undertake specific programmes.

Device Development and Manufacture

The device development and manufacturing team consisted of the members from the following areas:

- Inventor
- Device Engineering
- Packaging Department

- Analytical Chemistry
- Quality Assurance
- Supply Chain
- Supplier Injection Moulding
- Supplier Manufacturing Operations
- Consultant Clean Room Specialist
- Regulatory Affairs

The team completed the development of the device, provided clinical trial supplies and developed the supplier's capability, which included the introduction of cleanroom facilities and a quality system as well as the device moulding and assembly processes and preparation for a pre-approval inspection by the local authorities. Regulatory documentation was produced; quality standards for the device were established, and quality control (QC) inspection, test methods and release criteria were transferred to the release site.

The first step in the device development included a design review and a failure modes and effects analysis (FMEA). These steps established that the design met the performance criteria, but the FMEA did predict some potential quality issues in manufacturing. Corrective actions were planned and incorporated into the development programme.

Involvement and a high level of commitment from the supplier were critical to the success of this project. Early involvement of the local regulatory authority to define its requirements for both the device and the standards for manufacture was also considered essential, and the dialogue proved valuable to the outcome.

Clinical Development

The membership of the clinical development team was limited and consisted of the following departmental representatives:

- Clinical Development
- Regulatory Affairs
- Marketing

The team undertook the clinical trials, prepared the regulatory dossier and developed the labelling. Feedback from this team to the device development team was important, which was facilitated by the project core team.

Market Development and Launch

The membership of the market development and launch team consisted of the following department representatives:

- Marketing Department of the local company
- Business Development
- Art and Graphics
- Trademarks
- Supply Chain
- Manufacturing Operations
- Quality Assurance

The team developed the brand image, including trademarks and all packaging, developed pricing policy, planned the launch, prepared sales force training material and undertook the training and procured the launch supplies. The trade pack consisted of the device and one month's supply of the drug product.

Project Challenges

There were a number of significant challenges that the project team had to meet.

Time-Scale

The project time-scale was demanding; in September 1995, the team had 18 months to the target launch date. The team secured the first regulatory approval in April 1997—a considerable success given the other challenges on this project.

Resources

Company resources were limited. Consultants and contract staff were used whenever necessary, including QA, regulatory (to compile the dossier) and for supplies development (clean room and quality systems)

Clinical Trial Programme

A quality issue was experienced with the first devices used in the pivotal clinical study. Rapid diagnosis of the cause of the problem was made, and a decision was taken to stop the clinical study, withdraw the supplies and correct the issue before the trial was continued. The trial was resupplied within six weeks of the decision to stop it.

The delay to the programme was justified. The clinical development strategy required minimal patient numbers, which minimised the time for the completion of the trial. In these circumstances, it was considered that no issues would require explanation if rapid approval of the licence application would be obtained.

As a general rule in problem solving, any additional work required is likely to impact the project time-scale. Minimising the time to market necessitates consideration of the trade-off between progressing quickly to FDA/MAA (U.S. Food and Drug Administration/Marketing Authorisation Application) submission and the likelihood of prolonged approval times being encountered due to inadequate data.

Supplier

The inventor was responsible under the licence agreement for providing the devices. He chose a supplier who was excellent at moulding plastic components even though the supplier had no experience in pharmaceutical Good Manufacturing Practices (GMPs).

Geographical Location of Team Members

The team members were spread over a number of different locations in Scandinavia and the United Kingdom. During the development of the supplier's quality systems, the quality assurance (QA) team member was transferred to the United States.

Company Takeover

In October 1995, a hostile takeover bid was successful, and the company was sold. Over the next few months, the local company manager changed, and one team member left the company by the end of 1996. Also, the project leader was transferred to the United States in January 1997.

Success Factors

In spite of the challenges, this team met its objectives; however, there was almost three months' slippage compared with the

Figure 12.1. Rapid Device Development

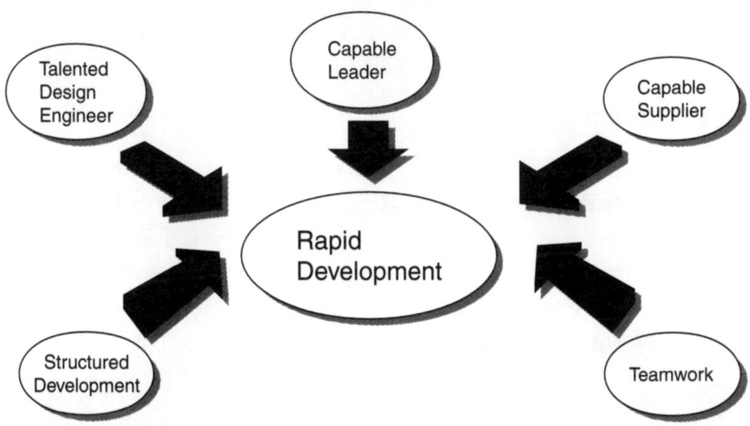

original planned approval date. The factors discussed below (Figure 12.1) were important in the team's achievements.

Team Members

The calibre of the team members was high without exception. The inventor of the device was a particularly talented engineer, and the rest of the device development team appropriately complemented his skills.

Leadership

The leadership was appropriate for the project. The leader was instrumental in the developing the objectives and planning and facilitating problem solving whenever issues arose. Communications were considered to be critical, and the leader took a very active role in ensuring that the core team communicated well and that the efforts of the subteams were well integrated.

Resources were reviewed every time an issue was encountered, and the leader and project champion worked well together to secure whatever the team required. This included additional manpower on occasions and some additional capital equipment to meet regulatory requirements.

Empowerment

The team members were of high calibre and had all of the skills required for success. The team was allowed to implement the project activities with minimal management interference.

Commitment

In spite of the change in company circumstances, there was a lot of energy and commitment within the team. The relationships between the team members were extremely good, and the supplier staff members were well integrated with the team. The supplier brought expertise in component manufacture and readily accepted help to develop quality systems and GMPs.

Figure 12.2. Structured Device Development

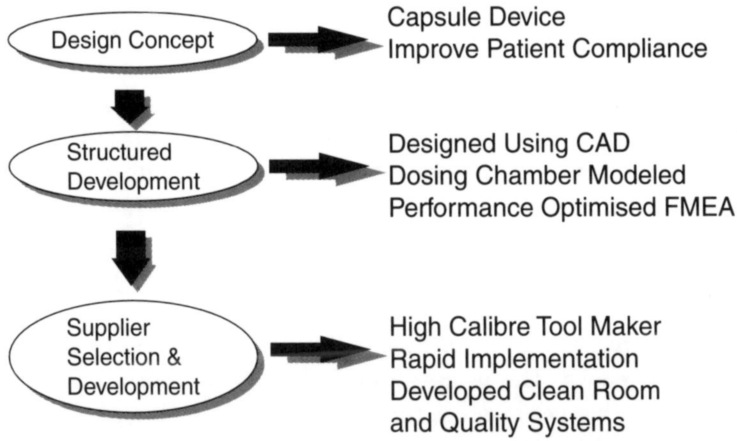

CAD = computer-aided design; FMEA = failure modes and effects analysis

Structured Development

Rapid development was achieved only through the use of structured development tools (Figure 12.2). The device was designed using CAD (computer-aided design) systems, and performance was established through the testing of models and computer design iteration. Design review and FMEA were very useful in optimising the design, and structured problem-solving techniques minimised development time.

CASE STUDY 2: RESOLUTION OF INTERRUPTION OF POST–LAUNCH PRODUCT SUPPLY

Background

A new product was launched in a major market in 1996, and subsequent launches were planned for 1997 and 1998 as licence approvals allowed. However, a major interruption to product supply was experienced in 1997 due to quality failures.

The product included a delivery device that developed performance failures. These failures started with complaints from the market. Eventually, batch rejections were experienced. The rejection level reached a point where manufacture was ceased until the device performance problem was resolved.

The device was purchased and assembled with one other component (purchased from a different supplier) in-house during the filling process. When the customer complaints were received, investigations were carried out by the device supplier and in-house. The supplier retested retained samples, reviewed manufacturing records and so on but could find no cause for the change in performance. The in-house assembly process was reviewed, and some changes to procedures were made which were expected to solve the problem.

As the incidence of the failures increased, it became apparent that the issue would not be resolved without the allocation of substantial technical resources to identify the root cause and to implement an appropriate solution. Therefore, a project team was set up to study the problem and recommend solutions.

Project Implementation

The project team had the following membership:

- Project leader
- Packaging engineers
- Analytical chemists
- Supplier device engineer
- QA manager
- QC chemist
- Production manager
- Purchasing and contract manager
- Consultants

Definition of Project Scope

The scope of the project was defined initially by brainstorming possible contributory causes. In parallel, the project leader commissioned a consultant to undertake a FMEA and a fault tree analysis of the assembled product. This analysis was considered necessary to understand all of the theoretical failure modes.

The initial project scope consisted of the following elements:

1. Review of supplier process
   - Changes
   - Performance tests
   - Release procedures
   - Process controls
2. Review of in-house process
   - Development data
   - Process changes
   - Performance tests
   - Trend analysis
3. FMEA and fault tree analysis

Project Strategy

The project strategy was to develop parallel programmes:

- To identify, as quickly as possible, any short-term measures that could solve the immediate problem and allow production to resume.
- To identify all root causes and implement programmes to prevent performance failures in the future.

Issues and Team Challenges

Cultural Issues

The project leadership and technical input from package engineering and analytical chemistry were allocated from a corporate,

U.S.–based, industrialisation function. The manufacturing facility was located in Puerto Rico, and the suppliers of components were located in France and Switzerland. A number of cultural issues arose as a result of this mix of nationalities.

- Language difficulties were experienced from time to time.
- Communication difficulties were exacerbated by the distances between corporate staff, suppliers and manufacturing.
- Puerto Ricans are proud people, and technical assistance has to be provided in a constructive and sympathetic manner.
- Leadership style needed to be modified for these different nationalities.
- The production team felt that they were unfairly feeling the business pressure for a supply problem that was caused by inadequate product development and industrialisation.
- The suppliers felt a certain amount of frustration since other customers had not experienced the same problem.

Product Development Strategy

For speed to market, the product development strategy determined that all components were available "off the shelf". No modifications were made to provide customised components or dedicated moulds and tools.

Some of the moulds had been in use for some time and performance drift was a possible contributory cause. Also, no specific functional requirement specification had been developed for the product (a combination of components). Specifications were set only on historical data.

Business Pressure

The interruption of supply at such a critical stage in the product life cycle resulted in a significant amount of business pressure. An extremely important role for the leader under these circumstances was to ensure that this pressure did not have an adverse effect on the project. A rapid solution was required, but the root causes had to be identified and resolved permanently. One potential difficulty with devices is that it is not always possible to predict the knock-on effect of apparently small changes in manufacturing or assembly processes. It was important, therefore, not to implement solutions that could cause different performance failures.

Management of the Project Issues and Challenges

The cultural issues were handled by good teamwork. The project leader put a great deal of effort into forming a team that worked well together and trusted each other. The manufacturing team, the supplier and the corporate technical staff could not be distracted by baggage from the past, and the causes had to be established without blame being attached to individuals or departments. The objective was to resolve the problem and ensure that other quality problems did not arise in the future.

The project team members were coached in the complexities of component interactions and process dependencies. They were encouraged to recognise that the problem was one of insufficient understanding of the product as a system of complex interactions and not the result of individuals failing to do their job properly. An open approach to information sharing was taken, and very frequent face-to-face contact between the team members was maintained. A partnership approach was taken with the supplier, not an adversarial one. This was a critical success factor in the rapid, short-term solution to the problem.

The project leader also set high technical standards for the project. Emphasis was placed on speed by getting it right the first time, by using rigourous experimental design and proving solutions adequately before implementation.

Corporate project team members were chosen carefully, both for their technical abilities and their interpersonal skills. Using technical consultants who had experience in fault diagnosis and in manufacturing development filled skills gaps. Again, the interpersonal skills of the consultants was an important success factor. The individuals took a coaching and guiding role, which helped significantly with the transfer of knowledge and the personal development of the other project team members.

The roles and responsibilities for the project team members were clearly defined. The team was also structured to facilitate project implementation. Two subteams were formed:

1. *Process team:* This team was responsible for collecting historical performance data and for the process review. All experiments were designed, additional test methods were developed and all testing was done for modified process parameters and components.

2. *Device component team:* This team followed up on the product FMEA and designed modifications to the components. Short-term and long-term improvement plans were developed and implemented.

Significant Project Findings

The following proved to be significant project events:

- A review of the development data showed that the product failures had been experienced earlier but at a very low incidence. The root cause was never identified due to speed-to-market pressures.

- There was no functional requirement specification for the product.

- The device supplier had refurbished a component mould, and the problem arose at the time of introduction of components from it. All specifications for dimensions were met, and incoming QC checks did not detect a change.

- The FMEA and fault tree analysis revealed a number of different possible failure modes, and a number of areas for improvement of the components were identified.
- A detailed review of the assembly process using statistical experimental design revealed process dependencies that were not previously recognised.
- The designs of certain other product components were found to be suboptimal, which had a cumulative effect on product performance.

In summary, the decisions that were made during development with respect to component selection and manufacturing equipment were made to facilitate speed to market, by purchasing off-the-shelf packaging and manufacturing equipment. Product performance was satisfactory at the time of launch, but the robustness of the product to process drift, both in-house and at the suppliers, was unknown. The performance failures were due to a quality change of one component because the product design was particularly fragile. This quality change in the critical component was not detected until product performance failures occurred. The specifications for components were set without sufficient understanding of the critical interactions of the components and their relationship to product performance.

Project Outcome

Changes to a number of components were made to make the product robust with respect to wear on moulds and normal process drift. Production resumed following the introduction of some changes to the assembly process and the introduction of one new component mould. This exercise took two months. The supplier had already started to make new tools for the component mould in order to increase production capacity. The complete improvement programme took over a year to complete.

The relationships which were developed during this project were very productive. One beneficial result was the establishment of a greater degree of trust between certain operations and corporate personnel and the development of a closer relationship with the device supplier.

Lessons to Be Learned for Development Programmes

The following lessons can be learned for product developments that involve devices and complex packaging components:

- A functional specification should always be developed for any product containing a device.
- This functional requirement specification should be used as the basis for developing all component specifications and tolerances.
- Design reviews, including FMEA, fault tree analysis and suitable tools, should be undertaken before the design is frozen.
- If compromises are made to meet time-to-market objectives, follow-up improvement projects should be run in parallel to avoid post-launch supply problems.
- Partnership arrangements should be developed with critical suppliers. The suppliers have expertise which can be used to the benefit of both the supplier and the pharmaceutical company.

13

Project Implementation

PROJECT PLANNING

Upon nomination of a compound into development, a project plan is required. This plan, in practice, takes several weeks to develop and is usually developed in more detail for the first phase, i.e., to the first decision point in humans, and in outline format thereafter. The use of template plans or model plans is common since project activities vary little from project to project; it is the details at the experiment and study levels that differ from one therapeutic area to another and from compound to compound.

An example of a high-level model Gantt chart is given in Figure 13.1. A model plan can be developed from the detailed work breakdown structure (WBS) given in Figure 13.2 (see page 195). Durations must be assigned to each activity in the WBS, and logic links added accordingly. Every development project will be dif-

Figure 13.1. Model Project Plan—Chronic Therapy

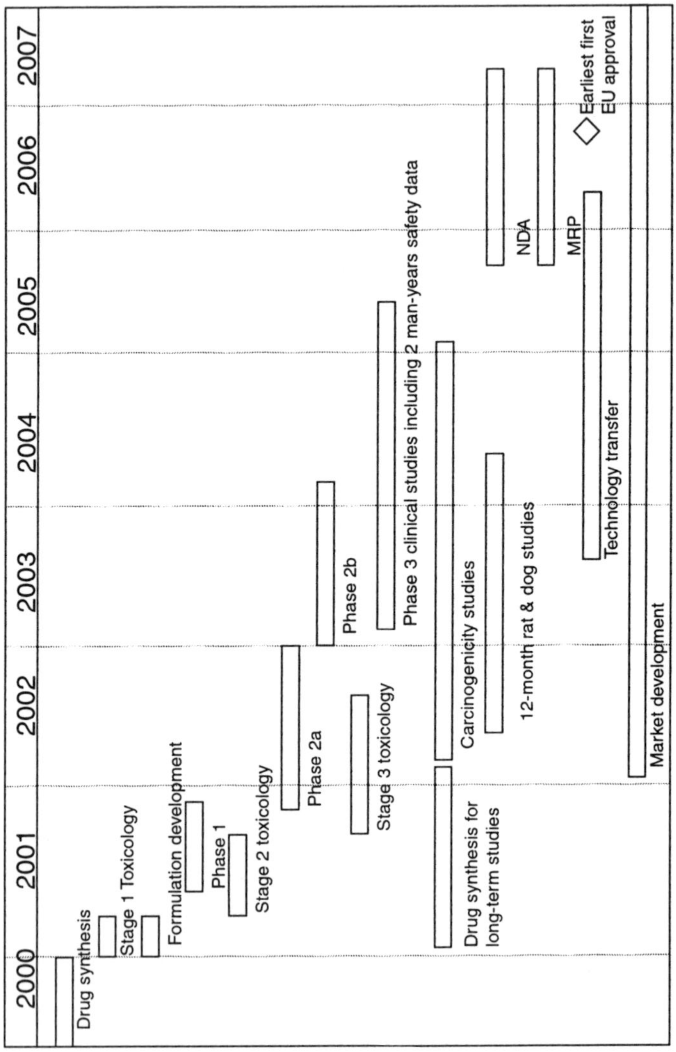

ferent in terms of the durations of the activities and in the order in which some have to be carried out. Not all activities will be required for every project. For example, acute indications will require neither long-term safety nor carcinogenicity studies.

The time-scales for project activities tend to vary from one therapeutic area to another. The time to complete a Phase 2 clinical programme for an anti-infective compound will be very different than for a central nervous system compound indicated for stroke. Hence, different template plans with different target time-scales for both exploratory development and regulatory development are very common.

Typically, the development plan will be a document consisting of the objectives and scope of the project and the decision criteria for at least the first decision point in humans. For the regulatory phase, the project plan will include the target profile, the minimal acceptable profile and a description of the preclinical, clinical and CMC (chemistry, manufacturing and controls) plans (see preceding chapters in this book). Time-scales will be identified for the major project activities, and target dates for all major milestones will be identified in addition to the key individuals responsible for their delivery.

Project planning software is increasingly used to plan projects and to track progress. Microsoft Project® is easy to use and is one of the most commonly used off-the-shelf packages. It is ideal because the software can be networked. It is easy to provide multiple users with read-only access to project plans at a number of levels, consistent with the work breakdown structure of the project.

Common Mistakes Made in Planning

Planning is an essential element of drug development. It is not an easy task to get it right—it is not even easy to define what getting it right is! For me, getting it right is to do sufficient planning to ensure that the project team has a clear understanding of what has to be done, by whom and by when. The result will be no surprises.

There are a number of common pitfalls that occur in the project planning process:

- No comprehensive overall written plan is prepared to summarise the objectives, team plans and roles and responsibilities.
- Some project planners love to create very detailed project networks with hundreds or thousands of activities and many complex dependencies. These become a full-time job to update and very quickly become disjointed from what is happening in the project. Team members find them difficult to understand, and the ownership is poor. A well-defined work breakdown structure and a milestone chart is more useful to the core project team than overly complex project networks.
- Plans created by planners not owned by the project team do not reflect what is really being done. Very detailed plans are best prepared and updated within a subteam, defining only those activities to be carried out by the subteam. This way the team will develop a plan with a level of detail that it feels comfortable with, and there will be a commitment on behalf of the team members to keep it up to date.
- A Gantt chart is not a plan; it is merely a summary of activities with start and finish dates (planned and or actual). A plan should include Gantt charts, but if these are the only documents available for a major project, it is a symptom of insufficient planning.

WORK BREAKDOWN STRUCTURE

The production of a work breakdown structure is helpful for planning, staffing and controlling a major project. A work breakdown structure is a top-down definition of the work packages required to deliver the project. A number of different breakdown methods can be used, for example,

- Work programme breakdown
- Functional breakdown
- Geographic breakdown

Work Programme Breakdown

The work programme breaks the project down into work-related packages, for example, drug synthesis, pharmaceutical product development, clinical programmes, preclinical programmes, and so on. This type of breakdown is cross-functional, since all related activities are included. Some examples are given below.

- The analytical methods development and testing required to support drug synthesis are included in this work package.
- Provision of clinical trial supplies will be included in the clinical programme.
- Purchasing and development contracts for manufacturing equipment will be included in the product and process development programme.

The high-level tasks for a work programme breakdown are described in Table 13.1.

Functional Breakdown

A functional breakdown assigns activities according to the organisational structure. In the example given above, the functional breakdown would result in the following assignments:

- The analytical methods development and testing for drug synthesis would be included in an analytical programme.
- Provision of clinical trial supplies would be included in the pharmaceutical sciences programme.

Table 13.1.
Development Project Work Programme—High Level Tasks

Project Managment
Drug synthesis
Safety pharmacology programme
Preclinical programme
Drug metabolism
Phase 1 clinical programme
Clinical development (Phase 2 and 3)
Phase 4 clinical programme
Pre-formulation
Pharmaceutical product developement
Process design
Process optimisation and transfer
Regulatory affairs programme
Market development

- Purchasing and development contracts for manufacturing equipment would be included in the supply chain programme.

Geographic Breakdown

All activities are allocated to a geographic region. This is particularly useful for clinical trials, marketing and pre-launch activities if it is used as an additional view of the project to the work programme version. It forms a simple list of activities for regional teams and, in particular, allows responsibilities to be clearly delineated from corporate roles or other regional team roles. For example, a work programme breakdown could be used to define the project up to the definition of the Phase 3 clinical programme, and a geographic breakdown could be used for the details below Phase 3 clinical studies.

For development projects, I have found that a work breakdown structure based on work packages rather than functional or geographic breakdowns is the most effective. However, since many project teams are international, a separate plan for a geographically defined group can be useful in adding clarification to roles and responsibilities and key project dates. A geographically defined subset of a work-based plan is the best way of achieving the simplicity desired.

Most work packages require multidepartmental input. Breaking down the work to individual departments will require many levels of breakdown; this creates too much detail to handle easily, and the overall shape of a project gets lost. For example, if a clinical programme is to be broken down to department level tasks, a clinical study will be broken down into protocol development, regulatory approval (Investigational New Drug [IND], Clinical Trial Exemption [CTX], etc.), the clinical phase (first patient entered to last patient complete), the statistical analysis and the report. For most planning purposes, it is sufficient to identify only individual studies with a start and end date.

The first level in the work breakdown structure defines the team structure:

- Project management
- Drug substance development
- Product design and development
- Preclinical programme
- Safety pharmacology programme
- Clinical programme
- Regulatory affairs programme
- Market development

Subsequent levels define the work packages and form the framework for the project plan.

A work breakdown structure does not reflect the order in which tasks have to be done; there is no definition of dependencies, and, therefore, there is no timeline associated with it. It does form the basis of the project plan. Assigning a duration to each task in the work breakdown structure and linking the tasks develops a project network.

A project network is a useful tool for project monitoring and progress reporting, but if the plan is too detailed, it becomes too complicated to update—the plan becomes a means in itself, not a tool to support the project team. An overall project plan which consists of activities at level four in the work breakdown structure forms an excellent basis for project monitoring. More detail can be held in plans developed by subteams.

The Work Breakdown Structure in Operation

Figure 13.2 shows a typical work breakdown structure for a development project.

Planning Organisation

Ten years ago, large central planning departments were the norm, and it was these staff who developed the project plans and schedules using expensive project management software. The plans contained hundreds or even thousands of activities, and project networks were produced with elaborate Gantt charts and multipage reports.

The plans were usually criticised for being out of date and not reflecting what was really happening in the project. The project team found the planning systems unwieldy and unresponsive, so little co-operation was given to the updating process. The planning department continued valiantly, updating and issuing the plans, but the business ignored them to a great extent.

The benefits of project networks and Gantt charts were recognised by many department managers, but the project management systems available required expert planners to use software that was difficult to use. Hence, central planning departments grew up and were staffed with experts who could compile complex project networks even though they were inflexible.

Many planners lost sight of the fact that a plan is not an end in itself. The plan should be dynamic, reflecting what is going on in the project. In order to keep a project on track, the milestones in the plan need to be achieved on time, but activities can and should change as problems arise and as corrective actions are taken to resolve them.

Figure 13.2. A Work Breakdown Structure for a Development Project

ID	ℹ	Task Name
1	**1**	**Project Management**
2	**1.1**	**Phase 1**
3	1.1.1	Appoint project team
4	1.1.2	Define project objectives and plan for Phase 1
5	1.1.3	Define Phase 1 go/no go decision criteria
6	**1.2**	**Regulatory Phase**
7	1.2.1	Appoint project team
8	1.2.3	Define product development strategy
9	1.2.4	Define target profile and minimal acceptable profile
10	1.2.5	Prepare development plan
11	1.2.6	Define go/no go decision criteria
12	**2**	**Drug Synthesis**
13	**2.1**	**Process Design**
14		Synthesis step 1
15		Synthesis step n
16	**2.2**	**Process Optimisation**
17		Synthesis step 1
18		Synthesis step 2

Figure 13.2 continued on the next page

Figure 13.2. continued from the previous page

ID	ℹ	Task Name
19	2.3	**Process Transfer**
20		Prepare transfer documentation
21		Sourcing study
22		Select site
23	2.4	**Contract Manufacture**
24		**Confidentiality Agreement**
25		Prepare and agree to contract
26		**Transfer Process**
27		Set up transfer team
28		Experimental batch manufacture
29		Evaluate material from experimental batches
30		Finalise transfer
31	2.5	**In-House Transfer**
32		**Provide Facility**
33		Specify facility requirements
34		Select contractor
35		Build or modify facility
36		Validate facility
37		Specify process equipment

Figure 13.2 continued on the next page

Figure 13.2. continued from the previous page

ID	ℹ	Task Name
38		Select equipment vendors
39		Develop supply contracts
40		Procure process equipment
41		Accept process equipment
42		Install and validate process equipment
43	2.6	**Transfer Process**
44		Transfer synthesis step 1
45		Process validation synthesis step 1
46		Transfer synthesis step n
47		Validate synthesis step n
48		Provide manufacturing documentation
49		Develop planned maintenance programmes
50	2.7	**Master Files**
51		Compile Drug Master File
52		Update Site Master File
53	2.8	**Analytical Support Primary**
54		Analytical methods development
55		Stability methods development
56		Analytical methods validation

Figure 13.2 continued on the next page

Figure 13.2. continued from the previous page

ID	ℹ	Task Name
57		Test method transfer
58		Stability programme drug substance
59	2.9	**Regulatory Documentation Primary**
60		Prepare IND documentation
61		Prepare NDA documentation
62	2.10	**Health & Safety Primary**
63		COSHH assessments
64		Safety and handling studies
65	2.11	**Packaging Development Primary**
66		Bulk container definition
67		Shipping studies
68	3	**Preclinical Programme**
69	3.1	Safety pharmacology programme
70		Study 1
71		Study n
72	3.2	**Preclinical Strategy and Plan**
73		Define preclinical development strategy
74		Prepare preclinical development plan
75		Stage 1 toxicology
76		Stage 2 toxicology

Figure 13.2 continued on the next page

Figure 13.2. continued from the previous page

ID	❶	Task Name
77		Stage 3 toxicology
78		12-month rat and dog
79		Carcinogenicity studies
80		Special studies
81		Prepare IND summary
82		Prepare NDA summary
83	3.3	**Bioanalytical Programme**
84		Bioanalytical methods development
85		Toxicology programme support
86		Phase 1 pK studies
87		Phase 1 support
88		Phase 2 support
89	4	**Clinical Development Programme**
90	4.1	**Phase 1 Clinical Pharmacology**
91		Prepare Phase 1 clinical plan
92		Tolerability/pK studies
93		Proof of concept studies
94		Prepare IND summary
95	4.2	**Define Full Clinical Development Strategy and Plan**
96	4.2.1	Develop clinical development strategy
97	4.2.2	Prepare clinical development plan

Figure 13.2 continued on the next page

Figure 13.2. continued from the previous page

ID	ⓘ	Task Name
98	4.2.3	**Phase 2 Clinical Programme**
99		**Phase 2a Studies**
100		Dose ranging studies
101		Dose regimen studies
102		Comparative studies
103		**Special Groups/Investigations**
104		Food interaction
105		Contraceptive pill interaction
106		Renal compromised patients
107		Hepatic compromised patients
108		Drug interaction studies
109		Prepare IND submissions
110		Prepare CTX/European clinical trials submissions
111	4.2.4	**Phase 3 Clinical Programme**
112		Pivotal study 1
113		Pivotal study 2
114		Long-term safety adult
115		Long-term safety paediatric
116		Local studies
117		Health economic study

Figure 13.2 continued on the next page

Figure 13.2. continued from the previous page

ID	ℹ	Task Name
118		Quality of life studies
119		Prepare clinical summary
120		Prepare European expert reports
121	4.2.5	**Phase 4 Clinical Programme**
122		Comparator 1
123		Comparator n
124		Special interest studies
125		Market seeding studies
126	5	**Pharmaceutical Product Development**
127	5.1	**Preformulation**
128		Physicochemical characterisation
129	5.2	**Product Development Phase 1**
130		Product design Phase 1
131		Process design Phase 1
132		Manufacture clinical supplies
133		Analytical methods development
134		Stability programme
135		Specifications development
136	5.3	**Product Design Market**
137		Formulation design Phase 2

Figure 13.2 continued on the next page

Figure 13.2. continued from the previous page

ID	ℹ	Task Name
138		**Primary Package Design Phase 2**
139		**Device Design**
140		Prepare user requirement specification
141		Prepare functional specification
142		Produce models
143		Performance testing
144		Market research
145		Design review
146		Failure modes and effect analysis (FMEA)
147		Value engineering
148		Ergonomic assessment
149		Finalise design
150		Finalise market product formulation
151		Finalise market product primary packaging
152		Finalise market product secondary packaging
153		Finalise bulk shippers
154	5.4	**Process Design**
155		**Process Design for Phase 2**
156		Select process Phase 2
157		Specify equipment Phase 2
158		Select process equipment Phase 2

Figure 13.2 continued on the next page

Figure 13.2. continued from the previous page

ID	ℹ	Task Name
159		**Process Design for Phase 3**
160		Select process Phase 3
161		Specify equipment Phase 3
162		Select process equipment Phase 3
163		**Specification Development**
164		Product specifications
165		Raw material specifications
166		Primary packaging specifications
167		Secondary packaging specifications
168		**Test Methods Development**
169		Analytical methods active
170		Analytical methods excipients
171		Analytical methods raw materials
172		Microbiology test methods
173		Packaging component test methods
174		Develop stability test methods
175		**Select and Approve Suppliers**
176		Select suppliers raw materials
177		Develop contracts
178		Develop raw material suppliers

Figure 13.2 continued on the next page

Figure 13.2. continued from the previous page

ID	ℹ	Task Name
179		Approve suppliers
180		Select suppliers packaging components
181		Develop contracts
182		Develop component suppliers
183		Approve component suppliers
184	5.5	**Process Optimisation and Transfer**
185		**Phase 2 Process Development**
186		Develop process Phase 2 clinical supplies
187		Transfer to clinical trial supplies
188		Manufacture Phase 2 supplies
189		Stability programme
190		Prepare IND documentation
191		**Phase 3 Process Development**
192		Sourcing study Phase 3 supplies
193		Select site Phase 3 clinical supplies
194		Build/modify facilities
195		Validate facilities
196		Procure equipment
197		Install and validate equipment
198		Optimise final process

Figure 13.2 continued on the next page

Figure 13.2. continued from the previous page

ID	ℹ	Task Name
199		Process scale-up one-tenth
200		Manufacture pivotal clinical supplies
201		NDA stability programme
202		**Process Transfer to Manufacturing**
203		Complete technology transfer documentation
204		Modify facility for full scale
205		Complete facility and utility validation
206		Specify any additional equipment full scale
207		Select additional equipment full scale
208		Procure additional equipment
209		Validate equipment
210		Scale-up to commercial batch size
211		Demonstrate process capability
212		Validate full-scale process
213		Prepare site for PAI
214		Manufacture/launch supplies
215		Postimplementation process review
216		**Test Method Transfer to Quality Control**
217		Provide transfer documentation
218		Train QC laboratory staff

Figure 13.2 continued on the next page

Figure 13.2. continued from the previous page

ID	ℹ	Task Name
219		QC method familiarisation
220		Problem resolution
221		Collaborative studies
222		QC accept test methods
223	6	**Regulatory Programme**
224		Develop regulatory strategy
225		IND, CTX, other clinical trials applications
226		Phase 3 clinical approvals
227		NDA preparation and submission
228		European MAA preparation and submissions
229		Japanese submissions
230		Other submissions
231		Labeling and text
232	7	**Market Development**
233	7.1	**Market Strategy and Planning**
234		**Develop Marketing Strategy**
235		Market analysis
236		Develop international marketing plan
237		Develop product positioning
238		Develop product differentiation

Figure 13.2 continued on the next page

Figure 13.2. continued from the previous page

ID	ℹ	Task Name
239		Develop key messages
240		Opinion leader liaison and advocacy development
241	7.2	**Develop Brand Image**
242		Trademark selection and testing
243		Logo development
244		Design packaging
245		Promotional materials
246		Public relations planning
247		Public relations implementation
248	7.3	**Market Research**
249		For segmentation
250		For positioning
251		For differentiation
252		For pricing
253		For branding
254	7.4	**Pricing**
255		Develop pricing policy

Planning has changed considerably over recent years. The availability of user-friendly personal computer (PC) planning packages has revolutionised planning and brought the capability of powerful tools to the bench-based scientist. So how can the new developments in planning tools be used to improve the project planning process without creating chaos with a plethora of plans and updating systems?

What are the needs of the organisation with respect to project planning?

- The project team needs an overview schedule of the major project milestones and activities.
- Department managers need detailed activity plans that show all of the department activities required to deliver functional milestones.

How can the planning organisation best meet these different requirements? A decentralised planning organisation can meet the needs of the project team and department managers, minimising the number of full-time planning staff involved. I have had experience in decentralised planning organisations which have worked well in some areas and not so well in others, depending on the commitment of the department manager and the aptitudes of staff assigned planning roles.

This decentralised organisation was composed of

- a small central planning office reporting to a project management function and
- function/department planners reporting in to the line functions.

The central planning office

- assigned a planner to the core project team;
- developed the work breakdown structure for the project, summarised activities and developed milestone plans; and
- updated the project plan and issued management reports.

The function/department planners

- expanded the work breakdown structure to a department level of detail;
- produce function and/or department plans;
- updated department plans; and
- issued progress reports to department managers, project team members and the planner on core project team.

Project Monitoring and Control

Effective monitoring and control is fundamental to the success of a project. Maintaining it on track with respect to time and scope requires excellence in leadership, science and teamwork. All projects provide their share of challenges to the teams. Problems and issues always arise, and it is the effectiveness with which these difficulties are handled which determines success, especially in terms of meeting time-to-market objectives.

Progress Monitoring

The project plan forms the basis for monitoring and control; however, it is nothing more than a forecast, and events will never proceed exactly as planned. The most critical aspects are the timings for the major project milestones, and project control should be concerned with maintaining these milestones on time. The team should be empowered to modify the project activities so long as these milestones are minimally affected, and functional management (Figure 13.3) must be prepared to revise resource inputs to resolve significant issues in a timely manner.

As project activities progress, the rate of progress must be evaluated and compared with the plan. Any deviations must be evaluated for potential impact on the finish date for the activity itself and future activities. For example, an issue with a stability study may be the result of an issue with a test method that can be resolved without impact on other planned activities. However, an issue indicative of instability with a formulation could have significant impact on the start of a Phase 3 clinical programme.

Figure 13.3. Project Management

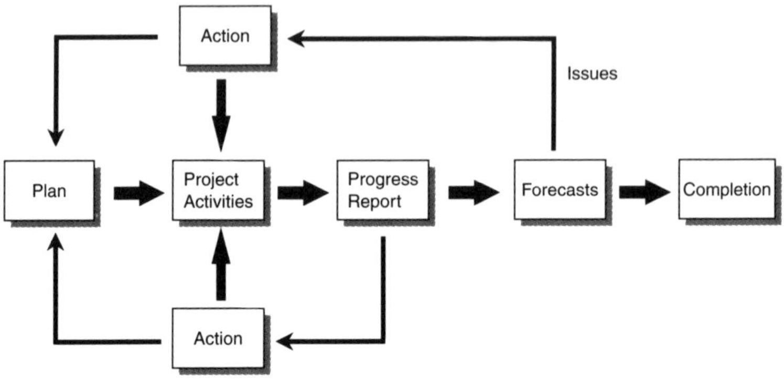

Clearly, early warning of issues is essential if their impact on the project is to be minimised.

In my experience, there are four basic causes for delays in projects. They are listed below in the order in which they have to be resolved:

1. Poor resource management
2. Poor project management
3. Insufficient scientific expertise
4. Unexpected and difficult technical issues to be overcome

Poor Resource Management. Insufficient resources lead to a number of problems if individuals are stretched too thinly; delays may occur if resources are not made available to start studies on time and progressed at the planned rate. Poor resource management can lead to some or all of the following issues:

- Individuals do not plan effectively, activities are not started on time or small tasks (such as ordering material, informing an analyst of which samples need to be tested to which specifications) are forgotten.

- Corners are cut in an attempt to expedite work, leading to the repetition of activities. For example, sample sizes may be reduced to minimise work, and equivocal experimental results may be obtained.

- The time to review protocols may be cut short, such that errors and omissions are not detected.

- Too much pressure on the best scientists can lead to mistakes and poor quality work.

- Too many long hours being worked by individuals to make up for insufficient staff numbers reduces morale and, ultimately, personal commitment.

I have seen very capable people criticised for poor quality work when the cause was not a lack of ability or commitment on behalf of the individual but of unrealistic expectations, given the amount of time or manpower available to complete a task. Poor resource management often results in staff being overworked, and morale suffers.

Good project leadership should minimise this type of issue, since resource requirements should be identified and agreed on before the activities are due to start. However, if the culture of the organisation is not one which supports good resource management, if there is not a good balance between the approved project portfolio and the resources available to do the work, if focus is not maintained, project teams will not be successful.

Project team members will work overtime, including weekends and holidays, to achieve certain tasks. Morale is usually very high when the pressure is on to meet a certain milestone. Successes can be celebrated and the team benefits from the experience. However, if this way of working becomes the norm, serious consequences can result, not only in terms of meeting project time-scales but also in the motivation of individuals and in the ability of an organisation to retain the best staff.

In his work, W. E. Deming showed that whenever there is a problem within a team, systems and ways of working will be at fault 90 percent or more of the time; only 10 percent or less of the time will an individual be at fault. As leaders and managers, it is our responsibility to provide the systems and support mechanisms for project teams to be successful. Good resource management, in my view, is one of the most important systems for successful drug development.

Poor Project Management. Good planning is essential if projects are to run on time. It is usually the fine details which cause delays. For example,

- excipients or packaging components not being available for timely clinical supplies manufacture;
- quantities of drug substance incorrectly calculated for critical path pre-safety or clinical studies; and
- insufficient time allowed or poor quality assurance (QA) liaison for timely review and approval of preclinical or clinical study reports prior to regulatory submissions.

It is important that the project team members have a good understanding of all the necessary project activities in order to complete the project milestones. It must very clear who is responsible for undertaking every task. The project leader cannot be expected to plan every activity, but the project subteams responsible for various programmes must communicate well, and the project leader should ensure that the appropriate mechanisms are in place. In particular, if specific individuals are identified as being responsible for each major activity, the project leader must follow up on every task.

The individual responsible for a particular clinical study within a programme must ensure that all of the following activities are completed on time:

- All pretrial activities are planned well in advance, centres are identified and the protocol is written.
- The protocol is approved.
- Investigators approve the protocol.
- Ethical committee approvals are obtained.

- Regulatory approval, IND, CTX and so on are obtained.
- Clinical trial supplies requirements are calculated and ordered. All contributors to securing supplies are informed in a timely manner of all requirements (drug substance, packaging components, comparator drug, placebos, etc.).
- Clinical trial manufacturing processes are defined and staff trained.
- Sufficient time is allowed for QA testing and release of clinical supplies.
- Stability data are available to provide sufficient shelf life to complete the study, or retesting is planned to extend the shelf life in a timely manner.
- Diary cards and case report forms are well designed and easy to understand.
- Doctors, nurses and patients are trained in how to take the drug, and training material is appropriate.
- Sufficient resources are available for centre monitoring.
- Patient entry is monitored regularly, and slow enrolment is followed up. If necessary, additional centres can be included.
- Any issues with the accurate completion of diary cards or case report forms are identified early and corrective action taken.
- The close down of centres is completed quickly.
- Communications between the biostatistician and the author of the clinical report are timely and appropriate.

Good communication is most important, since it is often poor communication between different departments that has the greatest potential to cause delays as a result of things not getting done on time. A good knowledge of regulatory requirements is required if delays are to be minimised in IND, MAA (Marketing Authorisation Application) and PAI (pre-approval inspection) approvals.

Issues and problems will always occur; therefore, early warning of events going off track and contingency planning are an essential part of project management. Last minute surprises must be kept to a minimum; when they do occur, rapid resolution is essential. The project leader needs to be able to evaluate risk, have contingency plans in place and know when to take risks to change the strategy to achieve a goal. Good teamwork is also important to implement changes to the plan effectively as required.

Insufficient Scientific Expertise. Each project team member must have the necessary skills to contribute to the project activities; inexperienced members must be well supervised. Good experimental design is essential to avoid repeating work and to generate the required information in minimum time. Understanding the data generated from studies and drawing appropriate conclusions is another aspect of scientific excellence which is vital for success.

It is the responsibility of department managers to ensure that the quality of the work undertaken by the team members is of the required quality. There is no substitute for scientific excellence. The culture, reward and recruitment and development systems must support the drive for excellence.

Unexpected Technical Difficulties. Technical difficulties will always occur and should be the only source of potential delays in a well-run and appropriately resourced project. Good leadership, scientific excellence, good problem-solving skills and excellent teamwork will ensure that technical difficulties have minimal impact on launch dates.

Progress Reporting

Progress reporting must be well managed. Progress should be honestly identified, but the project team must be given the opportunity to assess the true impact of any issues before conclusions are drawn on project timings.

The progress against project milestones is most valuable to communicate to senior managers, not progress against start and finish dates for all project activities, because these dates are the most susceptible to change. Clearly, changes to planned start and finish dates for major programmes are likely to impact on project milestones. Early warning of potential slippage will give senior managers the opportunity to revise resource allocations or take other action to minimise the impact, but the project team should be making assessments of impact and make recommendations accordingly.

Different individuals require different progress reports. Reports designed for the following categories of customers can be useful:

- Research and development (R&D) function heads and business managers
- Department managers
- Project core team members
- Project subteam members

Gantt charts showing current progress are a good way of keeping department managers and team members updated, but department managers will benefit by receiving a summary of the issues which have or may have an impact on departmental progress. Frequency of reporting is also important; too frequent updates will add a lot of noise to the plans. Subteams will obtain benefit from updating detail plans every two weeks during periods of significant activity; monthly updating may be sufficient at other times. Monthly reporting to the project core team is about the right frequency, even if the report is "no change".

Table 13.2 is a reporting format that can be very useful for monthly progress reporting for function heads and business managers.

Table 13.2.
Project XXX12345 Monthly Report

Project Leader: ______ **Project Number:** ______ **Date Issued:** ______

No.	Project Milestone	Date This Month	Date Last Month	Variance	Plan Date	Actual Date	Variance
1	1-month toxicology complete	—	—	—	Jan. 00	Jan. 00	none
2	Drug substance released				Sept. 99	Nov. 99	2 months
3	Clinical supplies challenge study released	Feb. 00	Mar. 00	1 month	Jan. 00		1 month
4	Start challenge study	Feb. 00	Jan. 00	1 month	Jan. 00		1 month
5	Challenge study complete	June 00	May 00	1 month	May 00		1 month
6	6-month toxicology complete	Dec. 00	Dec. 00	none	Dec. 00		none
7	Phase 1 complete	Dec. 00	Dec. 00	none	Dec. 00		none
8	Phase 1 review	Jan. 01	Jan. 01	none	Jan. 01		none

No.	Reason for Slippage	Corrective Actions

Other Issues

______

Project Manager

Index